No School Library Left Behind
Leadership, School Improvement, and the Media Specialist

Carl A. Harvey II

Linworth
Books

Professional Development Resources for
K-12 Library Media and Technology Specialists

Library of Congress Cataloging-in-Publication Data

Harvey, Carl A.
  No school library left behind : leadership, school improvement, and the media
specialist / Carl A. Harvey II.
       p. cm.
  Includes bibliographical references and index.
  ISBN 1-58683-233-6 (pbk.)
  1. School libraries--United States--Administration. 2. Instructional materials
centers--United States--Administration. 3. School improvement programs--
United States. 4. School librarian participation in curriculum planning--United
States. 5. Elementary school libraries--United States--Case studies. I. Title.
  Z675.S3H269 2008
  025.1'978--dc22

                              2007042178

Cynthia Anderson: Editor
Carol Simpson: Editorial Director
Judi Repman: Consulting Editor

Published by Linworth Publishing, Inc.
3650 Olentangy River Road, Suite 250
Columbus, Ohio 43214

Ideas and strategies used with permission from:
Lisa Hunt, GeorgeAnne Draper, Benita Brown, Alda Moore, Gwen Tetrick,
Sondra Patchett, and Barb Engvall

ISBN: 1-58683-233-6

5 4 3 2 1

TABLE OF CONTENTS

Table of Figures vi
About the Author vii
Acknowledgments viii
Introduction ix

CHAPTER 1: SCHOOL IMPROVEMENT 1
Definition 1
Implementing School Improvement 5
Professional Learning Communities 5
Why Do Library Media Specialists Need to Be Involved? 6
Focus on Assessment 7
Accreditation 8
Reflection 10
Professional Resources 10
Web Resources 11

CHAPTER 2: THE LEADERSHIP ROLE OF THE LIBRARY MEDIA SPECIALIST 13
School Improvement Snapshot 13
Be a Leader 15
Leadership Roles in School 16
Curriculum 16
Collaboration Tips for Standard .16
Resource Provider 17
Technology Leadership 17
Special Interest Groups 19
School Improvement Plan 19
Dissecting the Plan 19
Following the Plan 20
School Improvement Committee 21
Data Collection and Analysis 21
Technology Integration 22
Professional Development 22
Reflection 23
Professional Resources 23

CHAPTER 3: LITERACY 25
School Improvement Snapshot 25
Definition 27
Alphabetics 27
Fluency 27
Comprehension 28
Free Voluntary Reading 28
Writing 29

Table of Contents continued

Instruction 29
    Know the School's Reading Philosophy 31
    Gathering Information 33
    Love of Reading 33
    Adolescent Literacy 34
    Collaboration 35
    Writing 35
    Special Interest Groups 35
Strategies 36
    Alphabetics: Phonemic Awareness and Phonics 36
    Phonics and Phonemic Awareness Bibliography 37
    Fluency 37
    Fluency Bibliography 39
    Comprehension: Vocabulary Instruction 40
    Comprehension: Vocabulary Instruction Bibliography 41
    Comprehension: Text Comprehension 42
    Comprehension: Text Comprehension Bibliography 43
    Free Voluntary Reading 43
    Adolescent Reading 44
    Writing 45
    Writing Bibliography 46
    Research Process 47
    Copyright and Plagiarism 48
Collection Development 48
    Leveled Texts 52
Reflection 53
Professional Resources 54
Web Resources 53

Chapter 4: Mathematics 57
School Improvement Snapshot 57
Definition 58
    Number Sense 58
    Computation 58
    Algebra 58
    Geometry 59
    Measurement 59
    Data Analysis 59
    Problem Solving 59
    Trigonometry or Calculus 59
Instruction 59
    Match Maker 59

TABLE OF CONTENTS CONTINUED

Special Interest Groups 60
Strategies 60
    Number Sense 60
    Number Sense Bibliography 61
    Computation 61
    Computation Bibliography 62
    Algebra 63
    Algebra Bibliography 63
    Geometry 64
    Geometry Bibliography 64
    Measurement 65
    Measurement Bibliography 66
    Data Analysis 67
    Data Analysis Bibliography 67
    Problem Solving 68
    Problem Solving Bibliography 68
    Trigonometry or Calculus 69
    Trigonometry or Calculus Bibliography 69
Collection Development 69
Reflection 70
Professional Resources 70
Web Resources 71

CHAPTER 5: TECHNOLOGY INTEGRATION 73
School Improvement Snapshot 73
Definition 74
Instruction 74
Strategies 75
    Managing School Improvement 75
    Ethics 76
Collection Development 76
Reflection 76
Professional Resources 77
Web Resources 77

CHAPTER 6: DATA COLLECTION 79
School Improvement Snapshot 79
Library Media Specialist Role in Helping Collect Data 80
    Reports 81
Collectiong Library Media Center Data 81
Reflection 84
Professional Resources 84
Web Resources 86

TABLE OF CONTENTS CONTINUED

CHAPTER 7: PROFESSIONAL DEVELOPMENT 87

    School Improvement Snapshot 87

    Definition 88

    Instruction 89

    Strategies 91

    Collection Development 92

    Reflection 93

    Professional Resources 93

    Web Resources 93

CHAPTER 8: BEYOND THE SCHOOL 95

    School Improvement Snapshot 95

    Parent Involvement 96

        Family Night 96

        Library Media Center Web page 97

        Parent Collection 97

    Funding 97

        Reading First 97

        Improving Literacy Through School Libraries 98

        Other Grants 98

    Reflection 98

    Professional Resources 99

    Web Resources 99

Appendix A Staff Survey of Impact 100

Appendix B Student Surveys 103

Appendix C Collaboration Log 105

Index 106

TABLE OF FIGURES

Figure 1.1 State Department of Education Web sites 4

Figure 1.2 Accreditation Organizations 9

Figure 1.3 Connecting LMP to School Improvement Goals 10

Figure 3.1 Resources for Readers Theatre 38

Figure 3.2 Collection Development Resources 49

Figure 3.3 Leveled Library Guide 50

Figure 6.1 Data Collection Guide 85

Figure 7.1 Professional Blogs and Wikis 91

About the Author

 **Carl A. Harvey II** is the library media specialist at North Elementary School in Noblesville, Indiana. There, he is the co-chair for the school improvement committee, a member of the literacy committee, and the chair of the building media/technology committee. He sits on the district school improvement network, and is a part of the district accreditation steering committee. He is a past-president of the Association for Indiana Media Educators (AIME), and has served in various other roles including conference chair and Young Hoosier Book Award chair. He was the President of the Indiana Library Federation (ILF), and has served on various committees including chairing the ILF conference. He is also involved in the American Association of School Librarians (AASL) where he has served as the chair of the Affiliate Assembly and co-chair for the 2007 National Conference in Reno. He was awarded the 1999 Outstanding New Library Media Specialist and 2007 Outstanding Library Media Specialist by the Indiana Library Federation. For his work with AIME, he was awarded the Peggy L. Pfeiffer Service Award in 2007. He has published articles in a host of professional journals and is a co-author with Marge Cox and Susan Page of the book *The Library Media Specialist in the Writing Process* (Linworth, 2007). The library media program at North has been recognized with the Association for Indiana Media Educators Blue Ribbon for Exemplary School Media Program in Indiana (2005) and the American Association of School Librarians National School Library Media Program of the Year (2007). He also works part-time at the Speedway Public Library in Speedway, Indiana. For more information about the author, go to <www.carl-harvey.com>.

ACKNOWLEDGMENTS

This book would not have been possible had it not been for many special people. First and foremost to my mom and family who continue to support and encourage me with every new endeavor. Marlene Woo-Lun, Cyndee Anderson, Sherry York, and the entire team at Linworth Publishing, Inc., was amazing to work with; their guidance, suggestions, and support throughout the entire writing process was wonderful. The countless educators and library media specialists that I have had the opportunity to work with and learn from over the years have greatly influenced me – especially Susan Howard, Marge Cox, and Vince Barnes. They have taught me how to be a better educator, a better library media specialist, a better leader, and a better person. Lastly, but certainly not least, Karen Satterlee, who helped steer her student teacher down the right path in this field and continues to mentor him to this day.

Introduction

School improvement, state standards, student achievement, data-based decision making, accountability, and many similar words and phrases are among the popular vernacular in today's schools. Almost every decision made by administrators, school boards, and teachers focuses on the school improvement plan, process, and outcomes. Test scores are driving what is taught, how it is taught, and how it is assessed. Anything that does not directly impact student achievement and/or student test scores quickly can be deemed unnecessary and eliminated.

How does this impact the library media program? It impacts in every way and from every angle. Answer some of these questions from your perspective and then imagine the same questions answered by an administrator, teacher, or parent.

- Does the library media program impact student achievement?
- Is the library media program an extra or an essential part of the school?
- Is the library media program worth what it costs to maintain?
- Does the library media program have an active role in school improvement planning, implementation, and evaluation?

Administrators and schools boards have to see evidence that they are getting a high return on what can seem like an expensive investment. A library media specialist who participates in the school improvement process, demonstrates the critical role of the library media program in instruction, and impacts student achievement can create an environment where the library media program is essential.

The positive aspect of this age of accountability and standards is that the library media specialist has the opportunity to use these mandates as a vehicle to open doors to collaboration. Since teachers and administrators will be grappling with how to make gains in student achievement, this is a perfect opportunity for the library media specialist to demonstrate how the library media program can help. When the library media program becomes an integral part of the learning environment, teachers, parents, and students all will be willing to fight to maintain the program. They can become the biggest and best advocates for preserving the library media program. However, library media specialists have to step up and be ready to create those dynamic programs that students need, administrators support, teachers rely upon, and parents can see have a positive impact on instruction. In creating these programs, it becomes critical that the library media program is aligned with the school improvement plan. These plans drive many, if not all, of the decisions made in the school from instruction, to funding, to staffing, to anything in between.

In the pages that follow, library media specialists will find guidance in aligning their programs to the school improvement process. Chapter 1 will cover the basics of school improvement. What exactly is school improvement? Why should library media specialists want to be a part of it? Chapter 2 focuses on the leadership role of library media specialists. Library media specialists can no longer remain hidden behind the circulation desk; they must be highly visible in their schools as instructional leaders. State assessments focus heavily on literacy and math, so Chapters 3 and 4 respectively will look at these two content areas. School improvement also requires technology be an integral part of the plan; Chapter 5 will look at how technology impacts school improvement. Chapter 6 will examine data collection and analysis. Decisions in today's schools are based on data, so how do library media specialists collect and analyze this data? Professional development is a critical factor for school improvement plans, and library media specialists should play a critical role. Chapter 7 will provide some examples and strategies. Chapter 8 will highlight elements outside the school such as working with parents and funding opportunities and grants. Beginning with Chapter 2, the reader will also follow a fictionalized account of a school library media program and see how it is impacting school improvement. Each account is highlighted in a special box and entitled

"School Improvement Snapshot." Also, look for the big star throughout the book to find practical ideas and strategies.

No matter your views on data collection and testing and the school improvement process, the current reality has left little doubt that any of these things are going away anytime soon. The opportunities for library media specialists lie in helping teachers see how to take the data and the needs of the students and wrap them all together so that good learning opportunities are created. Take it past the drill-and-kill of test prep, and create real world projects and units that expand the students' minds. The by-product will be successful test scores, too. The opportunities are there.

Whether you are a veteran library media specialist or a rookie starting his or her first year, the intent is that this book will provide ideas and strategies that will help improve library media programs by making connections to the school improvement process. Reading this book will help create a mindset for library media specialists to begin thinking of their own ideas and strategies for impacting school improvement in their building. The bottom line is that successful library media programs impact student achievement, which is the whole goal of school improvement.

CHAPTER 1

School Improvement

Definition

The term school improvement has many definitions and connotations. For the context of this book, the term school improvement will be used in the broadest sense. School improvement is the process that schools follow to improve student achievement. Included under that umbrella are accountability (both for the students and the school), state standards, data-driven decision making, and community involvement in the school.

The attempt to reform and improve the U.S. educational system has been around practically as long as public education. A quick review of the last 25 years provides background knowledge of the current educational reforms behind school improvement. In 1983, *The Nation at Risk* was published. Commissioned by the U.S. Department of Education, this report blasted the educational system as being mediocre and declared that curriculum had been diluted <www.ed.gov/pubs/NatAtRisk/findings.html>. National and state lawmakers passed legislation mandating changes in education. The report called for "back to the basics" education, control of education by state government, and accountability. However, these efforts proved to deliver little effect. They failed because it was a top-down approach to change, and those on the practitioner level had little or no input, according to Richard DuFour and Robert Eaker's book *Creating the New American School*.

The next wave of reform was America 2000 promoted by President George H.W. Bush and amended by President Clinton. The eight goals were:

- By the year 2000, all children in America will start school ready to learn.

- By the year 2000, the high school graduation rate will increase to at least 90 percent.

- By the year 2000, all students will leave grades 4, 8, and 12 having demonstrated competency over challenging subject matter including English, mathematics, science, foreign languages, civics and government, economics, arts, history, and geography, and every school in America will ensure that all students learn to use their minds well, so they may be prepared for responsible citizenship, further learning, and productive employment in our Nation's modern economy.

- By the year 2000, the Nation's teaching force will have access to programs for the continued improvement of their professional skills and the opportunity to acquire the knowledge and skills needed to instruct and prepare all American students for the next century.

- By the year 2000, United States students will be first in the world in mathematics and science achievement.

- By the year 2000, every adult American will be literate and will possess the knowledge and skills necessary to compete in a global economy and exercise the rights and responsibilities of citizenship.

- By the year 2000, every school in the United States will be free of drugs, violence, and the unauthorized presence of firearms and alcohol and will offer a disciplined environment conducive to learning.

- By the year 2000, every school will promote partnerships that will increase parental involvement and participation in promoting the social, emotional, and academic growth of children.

<www.ed.gov/legislation/GOALS2000/TheAct/sec102.html>

The major new piece of this movement was the idea that all children can achieve and be proficient – a concept that is still debated to this date because of the measures used to determine if students are achieving.

With the 2000 election, not only did a new President come to Washington but also another attempt to reform the education system on a national level was introduced. President George W. Bush spearheaded the campaign for the federal legislative *No Child Left Behind Act of 2001*

(NCLB), which Congress passed. NCLB drives much of the school improvement movement in this country today. The four pillars of this legislation are:

- Stronger Accountability
- More Freedom for States and Communities (for spending federal funds)
- Proven Educational Methods
- More Choices for Parents

(<www.nclb.gov>). The phrase school improvement appears 84 times in the federal legislation. Many states have also adopted school improvement legislation. These state initiatives are direct attempts to meet some of the NCLB requirements to keep federal funding. Most state departments of education provide information for their state about NCLB and state initiatives on their Web sites (see Figure 1.1 for a list of state department of education Web sites).

The message from the legislation is clear that schools are expected to improve no matter what obstacles might be in the way. The school improvement process is a way for a school or district to work through those obstacles and toward meeting the benchmarks set in the NCLB legislation.

NCLB continues the practice of focusing on standardized testing results as a way to measure not only student achievement but also the success or failure of a school. Although there is no national test, each state is required to adopt an assessment tool and establish achievement levels. According to the legislation, by 2013 all students should be proficient on the state standardized tests for reading and math. Schools will be assessed each year based on their student scores. Benchmarks will vary from state to state, but schools must show Adequate Yearly Progress (AYP). Failure to meet AYP can result in stiff restructuring of the school, including removal of the principal and staff. Not only is AYP based on a total of all the students' scores but each subgroup, such as special education or English language learners, must also demonstrate improvement. NCLB attempts to provide federal oversight and demand accountability while at the same time give states some latitude. The debate continues on whether NCLB has been successful in that regard. The accountability written into the legislation is tied to federal funding. Each state has some influence in determining how a school is defined as reaching AYP.

STATE DEPARTMENT OF EDUCATION WEB SITES

Alabama Department of Education	http://www.alsde.edu/html/home.asp
Alaska Department of Education and Early Development	http://www.eed.state.ak.us/
Arizona Department of Education	http://www.ade.az.gov/
Arkansas Department of Education	http://arkedu.state.ar.us/
California Department of Education	http://www.cde.ca.gov/
Colorado Department of Education	http://www.cde.state.co.us/
Connecticut Department of Education	http://www.state.ct.us/sde/
Delaware Department of Education	http://www.doe.state.de.us/
District of Columbia Public Schools	http://www.k12.dc.us/dcps/home.html
Florida Department of Education	http://www.fldoe.org/
Georgia Department of Education	http://www.doe.k12.ga.us/index.asp
Hawaii Department of Education	http://doe.k12.hi.us/
Idaho Department of Education	http://www.sde.state.id.us/Dept/
Illinois State Board of Education	http://www.isbe.net/
Indiana Department of Education	http://www.doe.state.in.us/
Iowa Department of Education	http://www.state.ia.us/educate/
Kansas Department of Education	http://www.ksde.org/
Kentucky Department of Education	http://www.education.ky.gov
Louisiana Department of Education	http://www.louisianaschools.net/lde/index.html
Maine Department of Education	http://www.maine.gov/portal/education/
Maryland Department of Education	http://www.marylandpublicschools.org/MSDE
Massachusetts Department of Education	http://www.doe.mass.edu/
Michigan Department of Education	http://www.michigan.gov/mde/
Minnesota Department of Education	http://education.state.mn.us
Mississippi Department of Education	http://www.mde.k12.ms.us/
Missouri Department of Elem. and Sec. Education	http://dese.mo.gov/
Montana Office of Public Instruction	http://www.opi.mt.gov/
Nebraska Department of Education	http://www.nde.state.ne.us/
Nevada Department of Education	http://www.doe.nv.gov/
New Hampshire Department of Education	http://www.ed.state.nh.us
New Jersey Department of Education	http://www.state.nj.us/education/
New Mexico Public Education Department	http://www.ped.state.nm.us/
New York State Education Department	http://www.nysed.gov/
Department of Public Instruction (North Carolina)	http://www.ncpublicschools.org/
North Dakota Department of Public Instruction	http://www.dpi.state.nd.us/
Ohio Department of Education	http://www.ode.state.oh.us/
Oklahoma State Department of Education	http://sde.state.ok.us/
Oregon Department of Education	http://www.ode.state.or.us/
Pennsylvania Department of Education	http://www.pde.state.pa.us/
Rhode Island Department of Elem. and Sec. Education	http://www.ridoe.net/
South Carolina Department of Education	http://www.myscschools.com/
Department of Education (South Dakota)	http://doe.sd.gov/
Tennessee State Department of Education	http://www.state.tn.us/education/
Texas Education Agency	http://www.tea.state.tx.us/
Utah State Office of Education	http://www.schools.utah.gov/
Vermont Department of Education	http://www.education.vermont.gov
Virginia Department of Education	http://www.doe.virginia.gov/
Office of Supt. of Public Instruction (Washington)	http://www.k12.wa.us/
West Virginia Department of Education	http://wvde.state.wv.us/
Department of Public Instruction (Wisconsin)	http://www.dpi.state.wi.us/
Wyoming Department of Education	http://www.k12.wy.us/

Figure 1.1

Implementing School Improvement

What is evident by the waves of school reform at the national and state levels over the last 25 years is that a mandate alone will not improve schools. Real change happens at schools where the individuals in those schools take up the charge to make their school better. This is one of several critical factors in successful implementation of the school improvement process.

In their book *Creating the New American School*, Richard DuFour and Robert Eaker talked about factors that are needed to achieve significant school improvement. They focused on the people in the process. Effective principals and teachers who are leaders are critical. DuFour and Eaker also talked about a shared vision and a commitment to improve.

Victoria Bernhardt, in *The School Portfolio,* suggests an organizational structure for schools to collect data and organize it. Mike Schmoker, in his book *Results*, highlights creating measurable goals and collecting data. Allison Zmuda, Robert Kuklis, and Everett Kline, in their book *Transforming Schools: Creating a Culture of Continuous Improvement,* write about building a culture where everyone feels the importance of the process and actively participates.

All of these elements are building-based. A critical function for successful school improvement is that the teachers, support staff, parents, and administrators are the ones creating, implementing, and monitoring the plan. By working as a team toward a common vision and goal, these forces can help move their school toward reaching the mandates set by state and national officials. At the same time, educational opportunities for their students are improved.

Professional Learning Communities

Eaker, DuFour, and DuFour, in their book *Getting Started: Reculturing Schools to Become Professional Learning Communities,* share a model for small groups within schools to implement change. These Professional Learning Communities (PLCs) take the school-wide goals and focus on how their grade or department can help their students meet these goals. The focus is not on planning lessons for next week, but rather on the students and the specific interventions that will help students improve. This approach takes the overarching goal from the school improvement plan and breaks it down so that a small group of teachers (grade levels, departments, etc.) are looking at the school improvement goals and their specific students and determining actions to take to make a difference. Sometimes it may be a change in teaching method, or it may be trying to find ways to provide additional support and resources for the students. PLCs focus on working in a collaborative environment where everyone strives toward the common goal. The responsibility of success comes from working as a team rather than in isolation. Pooling people, resources, and knowledge results in collaboration to maximize the opportunities. This sounds very familiar to library media specialists, who have been working to collaborate with teachers for years, but the PLC concept expands the idea to include collaboration among all those in the learning environment.

Reading these books and others on school improvement, one can pinpoint that the connecting factors from all these experts are people, vision, goals, commitment, and data. School library media specialists can be critically involved in all these areas.

WHY DO LIBRARY MEDIA SPECIALISTS NEED TO BE INVOLVED?

School improvement impacts the entire school – every department, every teacher, and every student – and library media specialists need to be right there leading. From an instructional perspective, the information literacy standards – finding, evaluating, and using information – are all skills that students need to master before graduation. Beyond that, library media programs are at the heart of reading instruction by providing resources and motivation for students to become lifelong readers. Technology integration takes on new importance in the search for effective tools and strategies that help students learn, create, and imagine. In collaboration with classroom teachers, library media specialists work to embed all of this into the daily instruction. From an advocacy perspective, library media programs must be part of the solutions in making schools better. Library media specialists need to do everything they can to make sure the library media program connects to school improvement. With the current economic climate and the focus on standards and achievement, every aspect of schooling is under the microscope. Library media programs staffed by certified people and provided an adequate budget are not cheap. Administrators are going to have to see a return on their investment if library media centers are to maintain staffing and funding. For library media specialists, this means designing and aligning programs to enhance the school improvement plan. Library media specialists should ask themselves these questions:

- How do library media specialists impact student achievement?

- How does the library media program help the school meet the school improvement goals?
- How does the library media staff provide support and instruction that connects with school improvement?
- How does the funding of library resources and materials support the school improvement plan?
- Are there other ways library media specialists can use their talents to help? Organizing data? Technology integration?
- Is the library media specialist serving on the school improvement committee or other leadership team committees?
- Is the library media specialist effectively communicating to the principal how she impacts student achievement? To teachers? To students? To parents or community?

In the academic world, professors often use the phrase "publish or perish" regarding keeping on the tenure track. The same type of phrase "connect to school improvement or perish" could be used for library media programs. Library media specialists know that library media programs are a valuable and essential part of the school. It is critical that all the other key players in the game – students, teachers, administrators, parents, and the community – know that, too.

Dynamic Indicators of Basic Early Literacy Skills (DIBELS)
    <http://dibels.uoregon.edu>

Northwest Evaluation Association (NWEA)
    <www.nwea.org>

Focus on Assessment

Most standardized assessments of student achievement hinge on two core subjects – literacy and mathematics. Literacy encompasses both reading and writing. These standardized test scores become the benchmarks that the state and federal government use for determining AYP. NCLB legislation also requires testing of science beginning no later than the 2007-2008 school year at least once during the following grade ranges: third-fifth grade, sixth-ninth grade, and tenth-twelfth grade. While this testing is not part of what is required to figure AYP, Congress may consider adding it during the reauthorization of NCLB.

Annual formal state testing is summative evaluation giving data on the program and students. Summative evaluation is the final report and shares the success or failure of the program based on the data. Assessments given at the early stages, and periodically throughout, of a program's implementation provide formative evaluation. The data determines if the program is on track and moving in the right direction. Some of the data collected during the formative evaluation may be used to create the summative evaluation.

Many school districts want to do formative evaluation throughout the year and not rely solely on the state-mandated test. Northwest Evaluation Association's Measures of Academic Progress (MAP) testing and Dynamic Indicators of Basic Early Literacy Skills (DIBELS) are two examples of popular assessments that can be used throughout the school year. Because the results are almost immediate, the scores provide data that can be used to change interventions and instruction.

Beyond those developed by companies, many districts are also developing local assessments to determine if students are meeting the academic standards. Additional assessments sometimes can help paint a clearer picture than a test given once a year. NCLB dictates that by 2013 all students will be reading on grade level as assessed by a state standardized test (<www.nclb.gov>). This accountability element of the law has many schools focusing on literacy and mathematics to help their students meet this challenge. At some point there can become an overabundance of assessment. Schools have no control over some of these assessments while others can be decided on at the local level. The school improvement committee and school staff should take time to make sure that all of the assessments given provide valuable, usable data. Then, the group should see if they can find a way to replace or eliminate those that do not.

ACCREDITATION

Accreditation processes vary from state to state. Each local department of education determines how it will accredit schools. Accreditation is like a seal of approval. It goes beyond just looking at student test scores by looking at things like staffing, facilities, curriculum, instruction, and compliance with laws and rules governing schools.

Figure 1.2

Accreditation began as an initiative to provide credentials to colleges and universities. The accreditation allows these post-secondary schools to demonstrate that they meet high standards to be eligible for federal funds and that they are using these funds appropriately. The government recognizes six regional agencies to accredit colleges and university. Eventually, states began to see the need to accredit secondary schools and later elementary schools. Each state creates criteria for their elementary and secondary schools to be accredited. The six independent organizations that accredit colleges and universities saw this as an opportunity to expand and created divisions (Figure 1.2) that accredit K-12 schools. Many states will accept accreditation from these organizations as sufficient evidence that schools are meeting the state criteria for accreditation.

The largest of these accrediting K-12 organizations is Advance-Ed, which is the parent organization of the North Central Association (NCA) and South Association of Colleges and Schools (SACS). Covering more than 30 states across the country, NCA and SACS accrediting organizations merged in 2006 along with the National Study of School Evaluation to form one larger organization. While each group retains its individual identity, NCA and SACS now have a united set of standards and process for accreditation: Advance-Ed Standards for Quality Schools and Advance-Ed Standards for Quality School Systems. Advance-Ed Standards can be found at <www.advanc-ed.org/accreditation/standards/advanced_school_standards.pdf>.

CONNECTING THE LIBRARY MEDIA PROGRAM TO SCHOOL IMPROVEMENT GOALS

School Improvement Goal

Strategies Identify to Meet the Goal		

How can the library media program integrate, enhance, or provide support for these strategies working with students?		

What resources and materials can the library media program provide to support these strategies?		

Figure 1.3

The process school district and/or individual schools go through to gain accreditation is based on school improvement. NCA and SACS standards are based on a systematic approach to school improvement where all parts and components of the school keep working towards the common goal of improving student achievement. During this process, schools and districts are looking at data, implementing research-based strategies to improve, and collecting data to determine if the strategies worked. It is a continuous cycle. As part of the accreditation process, schools and districts examine if they have a structure in place to facilitate this continuous cycle.

REFLECTION

As library media specialists think about the school improvement process and the subjects that receive the most attention, they must begin to consider the role the library media program can play in this process. Reading the latest books, articles, and information about school improvement can help library media specialists be informed and educated when working with administrators and teachers. Chapters 2, 3, and 4 will provide some strategies and ideas on the role the library media specialist can play.

PROFESSIONAL RESOURCES

Bernhardt, Victoria. *The School Portfolio.* Larchmont, NY: Eye on Education, 1998.
DuFour, Richard, and Robert Eaker. *Creating the New American School.* Bloomington, IN: National Educational Service, 1992.
Eaker, Robert, Richard DuFour, and Rebecca DuFour. *Getting Started: Reculturing Schools to Become Professional Learning Communities.* Bloomington, IN: National Educational Service, 2002.
Evans, Robert. *The Human Side of Change.* San Francisco: Jossey-Bass, 1996.
Marzano, Robert J. *What Works in Schools: Translating Research into Action.* Alexandria, VA: Association for Supervision and Curriculum Development, 2003.
Reeves, Douglas B. *The Learning Leader: How to Focus School Improvement for Better Results.* Alexandria, VA: Association for Supervision and Curriculum Development, 2006.
Schmoker, Mike. *Results.* Alexandria, VA: Association for Supervision and Curriculum Development, 1999.
Wolfe, Patricia. *Brain Research: Translating Research Into Practice.* Alexandria, VA: Association for Supervision and Curriculum Development, 2001.

Zmuda, Allison, Robert Kuklis, and Everett Kline. *Transforming Schools: Creating a Culture of Continuous Improvement.* Alexandria, VA: Association for Supervision and Curriculum Development, 2004.

WEB RESOURCES

America 2000 Goals:
    <www.ed.gov/legislation/GOALS2000/TheAct/index.html>
The Nation at Risk findings:
    <www.ed.gov/pubs/NatAtRisk/findings.html>
NCLB Brochure from AASL
    <www.ala.org/ala/aaslbucket/aaslnclbbrochure.htm>
No Child Left Behind:
    <www.nclb.gov>

CHAPTER 2

THE LEADERSHIP ROLE OF THE LIBRARY MEDIA SPECIALIST

SCHOOL IMPROVEMENT SNAPSHOT

Parrott Elementary School is a medium-sized suburban elementary school. The student population is approximately 550 students in grades K-5. Due to staffing changes and retirements, the school plans to reorganize the school improvement committee this year. During the last few years, the committee has been collecting data and looking for ways to improve the students' standardized test scores. They have made some progress, but are always looking for ways they can get better. Susan Vincent, the principal, is hopeful that new faces on the team will help revitalize the group. She is talking with the retiring chair, Samantha Parker, and thinking about options for new leadership on the team.

Susan: Samantha, we certainly are going to miss you next year. Your leadership with school improvement has been very important to us the last few years.

Samantha: Thanks, Susan, but it is time to bring in some new people to the committee. It is always good to infuse new people in the process who might have a fresh approach or new ideas.

Susan: Any thoughts on who would be good to take over chair of the committee?

Samantha: Hmm.... Well, we could think about Karen Knapp, our library media specialist. Karen has been going above and beyond for the committee this year in her role as data chair. The charts, graphs, and spreadsheets she has developed and organized have really helped us to see where our strengths and weakness are as a school. She has a keen understanding of our school, and that is important as we think about a chair for the committee.

Susan: You are right about the great job Karen did with the data information this last year. I have also noticed that the work she is doing with teachers and students in the library media center has really focused on implementing some of the strategies our school improvement team suggested to teachers last year.

Samantha: She has that "whole school" perspective similar to your role as a principal because she works with every teacher in the building. She is well respected, so I think she would be a very logical choice for the position.

Susan: Thanks for sharing your ideas. I think you are right that Karen would be a good choice. I will ask Karen later this week if she would be interested in the chair position.

Later that week Susan talks with Karen...

Susan: Karen, do you have a couple of minutes?

Karen: Sure. What can I do for you?

Susan: Well, as you know, Samantha is retiring as chair of the school improvement committee this year, and I need to find a replacement. I was wondering if you might consider becoming the chair next year.

Karen: I am honored that you would ask, and I would be more than willing to be the chair of the committee. I know it can be a lot of work, but anything we can do to help our students be more successful is what we are all here for.

Susan: Great. We have made a lot of progress the last few years, but there is always room for improvement. I look forward to working with you in this new role. It will be a lot of work, but it should also be very rewarding.

BE A LEADER

If library media specialists want to impact school improvement, they have to be leaders in their buildings – just like Karen. Every building has leaders. There are formally identified leaders, such as the building principal and grade level or department chairs, but there are also informally recognized leaders – teachers who take the initiative to try new things, volunteer to head committees, and provide advice that is well respected by their colleagues and administration. Successful library media specialists work first with these informally identified leaders when building collaborative relationships. If these influential teachers buy into collaborations, they will encourage other faculty members to consult with the library media specialist. Working with those informal leaders builds bridges and increases the circle of influence. In a successful program, the library media specialist must become one of those informal leaders who are trusted by teachers, administrators, students, and parents.

Becoming a leader does not happen overnight, and sometimes it is a surprise when it happens. It takes time. It takes patience. It takes trust. It takes initiative. Library media specialists by the nature of their positions have an opportunity to develop into an effective leader in their building. Opportunities include:

- The library media specialist works with every teacher in the building and have contact with the entire staff.

- The library media specialist has a global perspective of the building. If the library media specialist makes opportunities to step beyond the library media center, the interactions with teachers, students, administrators, and parents provide insight into the bigger picture of the school climate, culture, and curriculum.

- The library media specialist's knowledge of the grade level curriculums in the building gives a depth of information that can be used when planning instructional opportunities. The library media specialist will be the first to notice gaps or overlaps.

- Library media specialists provide professional development – both formally and informally. The library media specialist can be the "go-to" person when the staff needs information, training, resources, etc.

If library media specialists seize these opportunities, they can become leaders – people teachers and administrators can depend upon. They can build a level of trust where people are free to share their ideas, thoughts, and feelings. A library media specialist who has demonstrated himself as a leader in the building has just added another reason why his library media program is a critical part of the school. An important by-product of this leadership role is gaining allies who are convinced that library media centers are important.

LEADERSHIP ROLES IN THE SCHOOL

CURRICULUM

As the school improvement movement has strengthened, states across the country have turned their curriculum guides into academic standards. These standards have become the defining objectives for each subject and grade levels – both for assessment at the local level and as the measurement for success on statewide standardized testing.

Some states, such as Kansas, have developed specific standards for library media (www.kerc-ks.org). Other states have decided not to have specific library standards. Indiana, for examples, has correlated the American Association of School Librarians (AASL) Information Literacy Standards with the Indiana Academic Content Standards (www.doe.state.in.us/standards/ILS_Correlations.html). Library media specialists need to be aware of the standards in use in their state and use them as they co-plan, co-teach, and co-assess with teachers. Demonstrating the connections between information literacy and academic standards provides a connection for collaboration. Documenting how students are meeting academic standards and how the library media program is helping to support these standards is critical.

COLLABORATION TIPS FOR STANDARDS

Library media specialists need to familiarize themselves with the content standards in the subjects and grade levels their building serves. While the classroom teacher should be the expert on their standards and the library media specialist should be the expert on the information literacy standards, each should be at least familiar with the standards of the other.

One solution is to keep a binder at one's desk with the standards grouped by subject and grade level. Take this when planning with teachers and refer to the standards to make focused instructional outcomes for students. You might also have the standards downloaded on a laptop and take it with you when planning.

As teachers work to create or revise themes or units of study, the library media specialists' knowledge of the standards and curriculum across the grade levels can provide focus and avoid including material and resources meant for another grade level or content area. The standards guide all instruction in the building, so it is crucial that library media specialists take the time to become well versed in the standards. School improvement plans focus on literacy and mathematics, so the library media specialist will want to be keenly aware of the standards in these particular areas. Knowing the standards will provide opportunities and ideas for collaboration.

Almost every decision the library media specialist makes should be tied back to school improvement. As part of our curriculum role, library media specialists should be looking at the school improvement plan and looking for ways to help reach those goals. For example, when planning with teachers, the library media specialist can offer suggestions for projects and lessons that directly support the school improvement goals.

RESOURCE PROVIDER

In addition to the instructional role, potential for impacting student achievement also carries over into another role of the library media specialist – resource provider. Materials should be selected so that teachers and students have books, videos, Web sites, etc., that will meet the content standards. For example, if the school is working on mathematical computation, the library media specialist would work to purchase books and manipulatives, collect Web sites for students and teachers, and look for other information resources to support teaching and learning.

Curriculum, instruction, and assessment are three important components of the school. They dictate what is taught, when it is taught, how it is taught, and how and when it is assessed. Library media specialists should be at the forefront of helping to develop instructional opportunities for students that ensure information literacy skills are embedded in that instruction.

TECHNOLOGY LEADERSHIP

The rapid influx of technology over the last several decades has made an impact on today's students and how they learn. Students cannot remember a time when there was not cable television, the Internet, or cell phones. Over the years there have been, and unfortunately, probably will continue to be, fiercely fought turf wars between technology specialists and library media specialists. For library media specialists to be leaders in this area, they have to be diplomats. Just as library media specialists have developed skills in working with all types of teachers, they need to transfer those skills to working with technology departments.

In some buildings the library media specialist is the prime connection between technology and instruction. Other schools may have district trainers who work with teachers on technology integration. Purchasing decisions may rest with the building principal or be made by a director of technology at the central office level. However the technology administrative structure is set up at the school or district, it is important for the library media specialist to be an active part of the process.

The global perspective of the school environment plays a critical part in the library media specialist's role in technology leadership. They can see what technology tools and resources are available currently or should be purchased to help the school meet its school improvement goals. The library media specialist can see what technology tools teachers are using or not using, too. They can tell when teachers are frustrated, angry, or excited about using technology. This information becomes especially important in planning professional development and making purchasing decisions. For example, in some districts, the library media specialist may have to work with a building principal, director of technology, director of media services, district technology specialist, and a building media/technology advisory committee. All of these people have their "I want" and "I need." The library media specialist has to be able to work with all these groups successfully and can be the common denominator among them. The library media specialist can also help the group focus on the students and school improvement when making decisions.

People skills are critical, and this is where the leadership role comes into play. As the middle point among all these interest groups, the library media specialist can help the director of technology understand the needs of the building and at the same time explain to the building media/technology advisory team why a decision was made at the district level. The library media specialist wants all those groups to see him or her as someone on which to rely for information and for input in decision-making and as a leader in integrating technology.

Library media specialists should be modeling using technology with students. They should be helping teachers see how they can use these resources effectively. Library media specialists need teachers to see how to avoid frustration, how to be flexible, and how to be comfortable using technology. If people learn they can depend on them, the library media specialist can exert a great deal of influence.

SPECIAL INTEREST GROUPS

As part of *No Child Left Behind* (NCLB) all subgroups must meet the high standards each state sets – this includes special education students and English language learners. Library media specialists can use this as an opportunity to collaborate with the special education teachers. When they are working in small groups or in self-contained classrooms, are there potential opportunities for the special education teacher and the library media specialist to work together? For English language learners, resources are going to be critical. What can the library media specialist provide in the collection to help support these learners? When designing projects with classroom teachers, how can the library media specialist keep English language learners and special education students in mind so they can be successful with the project, too?

School Improvement Plan

DISSECTING THE PLAN

School improvement plans contain several key pieces of information. If the library media specialist is part of the team that writes the plan, often the library media program can be written right into the plan. Not all school improvement plans are exactly the same, varying from state to state on what items are required to be included. Some possible sections:

- Goal(s) that is measurable
- Data to support choice of goal
- Data to be collected to determine if the goal is successful
- Interventions
- Research/Best practices
- Resources
- Assessments
- Instructional strategies
- Technology integration strategies
- Professional development

One district took the technology integration strategies one step farther and created a heading for media and technology strategies. Every school in that district not only had technology strategies for meeting the goal but also library media strategies.

FOLLOWING THE PLAN

⭐ As schools implement new instructional programs to impact school improvement, library media specialists should find ways to use those new programs in their library media centers. For example, a district might have a writing consultant helping teachers improve instruction in writing. As the teachers are trained, the library media specialist should participate in the training sessions. If the library media specialist is not on the list to be trained, take the initiative and ask to be included. Students in the library media center need to hear the same vocabulary and experience the same instructional techniques used in the classroom. Administrators notice when library media specialists are enthusiastically participating as part of the solution. In addition, teachers see library media specialists as colleagues facing the same challenges when training is shared.

⭐ If part of the school improvement plan contains ideas such as each classroom will have a word wall or each classroom will post the problem-solving process, make sure those items are also visible in the library media center. As part of one school improvement plan, one of the strategies was to use the Big6 Research model with students while researching. Each teacher in the building posted a sign of the Big6 for students to refer to while in the classroom as well as the library media center.

⭐ Be intentional with making connections to school improvement. In the library media center newsletter highlight collaborative projects and how they are connecting to the school improvement plan. When sending out suggestions for new read-alouds or books that teachers should know about, add a line at the bottom of the e-mail that shows how this book would connect to the school improvement plan. When sharing Web sites with staff, highlight how it connects to the school improvement plan. Making these connections shows everyone who sees those e-mails or newsletters that the library media program is focused on school improvement.

School Improvement Committee

At a minimum, the library media specialist should be a member of the school improvement committee. Most schools have teachers, administrators, parents, and community members serving on the team. Some reasons that library media specialists make good school improvement committee members include:

- The library media specialist is especially positioned to be a valuable voice at the table.
- The library media specialist works with every teacher in the building and provides resources and instruction at all grade levels to meet curriculum and standards.
- The librarian never gets wrapped up in a specific grade level or subject area. In contrast, the library media specialist has a global perspective and is aware of issues and concerns that affect the whole school.

Schools differ on how the school improvement team is formed. The members may come from principal appointments, or perhaps the teachers' union is responsible for selecting the committee members. In every instance, the library media specialist should clamor to be first in line to volunteer. The role a library media specialist plays on the school improvement team can vary. Possibilities include:

- Data collection and analysis
- Technology integration
- Professional development
- Chair

The talents and strengths of the library media specialist will dictate what role he or she plays on the team, but the important thing is that the library media specialist is part of the process.

DATA COLLECTION AND ANALYSIS

Data collection and analysis is the heart of the school improvement plan. Data starts the process by determining what areas are in need of improvement. Then research and the data that supports that research determine what strategies to implement for improvement. Finally, data determines whether the strategies were successful or not. With data it is important to collect and organize it well. A library media specialist who is skilled in organizing information can work to develop spreadsheets and data collection tools to make the process easier. Library media specialists can also use their information-seeking and gathering skills to find research to help the school improvement committee make informed decisions on what instructional strategies to implement.

TECHNOLOGY INTEGRATION

Most school improvement plans must also demonstrate how technology can help reach the goal. Library media specialists, who are catalysts for technology integration in their schools, should be guiding and aiding in brainstorming ideas of how technology can help meet the school improvement goals. In this area, an opportunity exists for library media specialists to ensure information literacy strategies are included in any plan.

PROFESSIONAL DEVELOPMENT

The school improvement plan provides direction for professional development. Library media specialists, especially those who attend professional development meetings in their field, can be especially adept at finding people to lead professional development seminars that will further the school improvement plan's objectives. A library media specialist's knowledge of the staff and curriculum make her attuned to the needs of the building. The library media specialist's role as a teacher also makes him a prime candidate for providing training to teachers as well. For example, the library media specialist might present an in-service on using the software Inspiration™ to teach prewriting. The in-service might be focused on how using this software could help with one of the school improvement goals.

One of the goals of the library media specialist is to be seen as an instructional leader in the building. By working with every teacher and the administrator, library media specialists build trusting relationships. This level of trust is crucial for successful collaborative projects and activities. Administrators will recognize a library media specialist who has built these positive relationships of respect and trust as an effective leader. Those are the types of leaders who can guide the staff through the school improvement process by chairing the committee.

REFLECTION

Think about the interactions a library media specialist has with a principal. The other day the principal walked into the library media specialist's office. He took a seat in the extra chair next to the desk. For the next 30 minutes, the conversation centered around school improvement. They decided what data to track from the new district assessment and how to do that easily and effectively. They probably got sidetracked a couple of times in the conversation, but the conversation always came back to school improvement.

Honestly, it does not really matter what the conversation covered. What *is* important is that the principal valued the library media specialist's input and ideas and wanted to have the library media specialist involved in creating solutions. That principal realizes the potential he has with his library media specialist. They can easily share and discuss things because they have figured out they have similar perspective – a whole-school perspective.

Opportunities for leadership for the library media specialist are many. Library media specialists have to take the initiative when it comes to becoming a leader in their school and in school improvement, because those will be critical elements in creating successful and thriving library media programs.

PROFESSIONAL RESOURCES

Anderson, Mary Alice. "Leadership: What Makes Us Tick?" *Library Media Connection* March 2006:14-19.

Buzzeo, Toni. "Collaborating from the Center of the School Universe." *Library Media Connection* January 2006:18-20.

Buzzeo, Toni. *Collaborating to Meet the Standards (K-6).* 2nd ed. Worthington, OH: Linworth Publishing, Inc., 2007.

Hartzell, Gary. *Building Influence for the School Librarian: Tenets, Targets, and Tactics.* Worthington, OH: Linworth Publishing, Inc., 2003.

Harvey II, Carl A. "Impacting School Improvement." *Library Media Connection* March 2006.

Johnson, Doug. *Indispensable Librarian.* Worthington, OH: Linworth Publishing, Inc., 1997.

Lankford, Mary. *Leadership and the School Librarian: Essays from Leaders in the Field.* Worthington, OH: Linworth Publishing, Inc., 2006.

Nichols, Beverly, Sue Shidaker, Gene Johnson, and Kevin Singer. *Managing Curriculum and Assessment: A Practitioner's Guide.* Worthington, OH: Linworth Publishing, Inc., 2006.

Repman, Judi, and Gail Dickinson, ed. *School Library Management.* 6th ed. Worthington, OH: Linworth Publishing, Inc., 2007.

CHAPTER 3

Literacy

School Improvement Snapshot

We return to Parrott Elementary where the School Improvement Committee is meeting. They are discussing the recently returned results of the state standardized tests. Those in attendance are:

- Karen Knapp, library media specialist and chair
- Samantha Parker, past-chair and fourth grade teacher
- Margie Preston, math subcommittee chair and first grade teacher
- Patrick Patterson, literacy subcommittee chair and second grade teacher
- Grace Williams, kindergarten teacher
- James Matthews, fifth grade teacher
- Laura White, special education teacher
- Walter Samuels, parent and community member
- Susan Vincent, principal

Karen: Welcome to today's meeting. We are going to focus on the literacy results on the state test. Patrick, can you give us an update?

Patrick: Yes, our committee and each grade level PLC (professional learning community) has been analyzing the results. Overall we are very pleased with our test scores. We find that we are doing very well in the areas of vocabulary and phonics. Our comprehension scores were good, too, except for one area – informational text.

Laura: Yes, our special education team has noticed that a lot of students struggle when moving from fictional text to informational text.

Grace: So what do we need to do about these results? The data is clearly telling us we need to revamp our teaching strategies at all grade levels. I know I want to talk with the other kindergarten teachers about how we might include more non-fiction text in our classrooms.

Karen: I can help with that. As we are working on your units, I can help find appropriate titles in our collection that will meet your needs.

Patrick: That is great. But, I think this is more than just finding more titles. We need to work on specific skills to help our students understand how to read and comprehend informational text.

Karen: Patrick is absolutely right. From my perspective in the library media center, I can see us doing some mini-lessons before each research project with each grade level. The mini-lessons can focus on strategies for reading informational text. As I work with teachers, I will encourage them, based on these results, to include time for these strategies in our projects. I think it not only could make a big impact on our scores but also would help our students be better readers of informational resources during research projects.

Karen has taken the initiative in suggesting how the library media program can offer support to a struggling area of literacy in her school. She will use this information as she is planning with teachers. It can be very powerful as part of a planning session for a library media specialist to say, "As we noted on our standardized tests, we need to work on informational text, and this would be a great opportunity to incorporate a few lessons on how to work with informational text before we start our new research project."

Definition

Literacy is a huge, all-encompassing term and can include information literacy and media literacy. For the context of this book, the major focus will be the skills necessary for reading and writing. The National Reading Panel (NRP) was commissioned by Congress to study research about reading. The NRP was convened by the National Institute of Child Health and Human Development in consultation with the U.S. Department of Education. The panel presented their findings in April 2000. Based on their research, the study concluded that phonemic awareness, phonics, fluency, and comprehension were the most effective strategies for teaching students reading. In addition, this chapter will also discuss free voluntary reading and writing as part of literacy.

ALPHABETICS

Alphabetics includes both phonemic awareness and phonics. Phonemic awareness is the ability to see, think, and work with individual sounds in a spoken word. For example, the words dog, dead, and day all start with the /d/ sound. Phonemic awareness is one of the best predictors of success in learning to read. Phonics is teaching the relationships between letters and sounds. As students learn the relationships between sounds and letters, they have a starting place for decoding unfamiliar words (*Report*)

FLUENCY

Fluency focuses on how accurately and quickly a reader reads. Fluency is a bridge from instruction and comprehension (Gambrell, Morrow, and Pressley, 204) Fluent readers are able to automatically recognize words. Readers should be able to not only recognize the words quickly but also almost effortlessly and instantly. The more the readers focus on decoding, the less focus can be placed on comprehension. As students get faster at decoding, they then have more capacity for working on comprehension (Gambrell, Morrow, and Pressley, 205).

Fluent readers use inflection and emotion in their reading. They use intonation, stress, tempo, and appropriate phrasing when reading aloud. When students demonstrate the emotion in their reading it is a signal of comprehension as well (Gambrell, Morrow, and Pressley, 205).

COMPREHENSION

The NRP included in this heading vocabulary instruction and text comprehension. Students learn and work with vocabulary in a variety of activities in the classroom each day. From learning a new word in a story to a mini-lesson on how to avoid using the same word over and over in their writing, there are countless times when students will be digesting new words and their meanings. Even more, students will be learning new words for new concepts they are learning in each and every subject. For example, the steps in a research process would require students to learn the word for each step and what that word means in context to the research process (Gambrell, Morrow, and Pressley, 179). There are two types of vocabulary – oral and print. When readers come to a word they don't know, they can decode it transferring it to oral vocabulary. Words that are in the oral vocabulary then can be understood by the reader. So the larger the students' vocabulary, the better reader they will be (*Report*).

Reading is an interaction. To comprehend text, students must be able to not only figure out what the word is but also process what the word means. Students take what they are reading and relate that to their past experiences and knowledge (*Report*). Comprehension is the end goal of reading instruction. Beyond just fiction, today's students need strategies for comprehending a variety of genres and formats including informational text. Direct instruction for comprehension should provide students with a toolbox of ideas and strategies that can use independently to comprehend text (Gambrell, Morrow, and Pressley, 221).

FREE VOLUNTARY READING

Dr. Steven Krashen, emeritus professor of education at the University of Southern California, argues in his book, *The Power of Reading,* that the National Reading Panel left out a major element of instruction – in-school Free Voluntary Reading. The report does not rule out that Free Voluntary Reading may have an impact, but rather contends the research is not there yet to prove it is an effective instructional strategy.

Free Voluntary Reading includes self-selected reading, sustained silent reading, and extensive reading. Self-selected reading is a block of time used for student choice reading during the language arts instruction period. Sustained silent reading is when everyone – including the teacher – takes a break and reads something of their choice. Extensive reading requires readers, after they have read something of their own choice, to do an activity such as write a short summary or something. The key factor in whatever form of free voluntary reading is that students are reading materials of their own choice (Krashen, 87).

WRITING

As students develop their literacy skills of reading the written word, it also is important that they learn to use language to create their own writing to share with readers. Writing can be intended for a variety of audiences and in a variety of formats. Student writing skills evolve just as reading skills do.

Most state assessments require students to be able to write based on a provided prompt. Reading and writing are interlinked since students need to be able to read fluently in order to write effectively. Wide reading enriches writing by providing students with models of good writing, possible examples to use, a broader view of problems, and an effective vocabulary. Students who read well are also better able to research and write. P. David Pearson, professor and dean at the University of Berkley, makes the connection between reading and writing at an early age. He says that as kids are writing in kindergarten and younger, they are spelling words as they sound, which sets them on a course for learning phonemic awareness (Pearson, 6). Students also begin to make connections with sounds to letters, which is a basis of phonics. So, as students are writing they are also learning to read because the two process work in tandem.

INSTRUCTION

Ask some of the following questions:
- What does the library media specialist know about teaching reading?
- What does the library media specialist know about how reading is taught in his building?
- How can the library media program make an impact on reading instruction?
- What does the library media specialist know about teaching writing?
- What does the library media specialist know about how writing is taught in her building?
- How can the library media program make an impact on writing instruction?

The primary role of a library media specialist is that of a teacher. Findings in the Alaska study by Dr. Keith Curry Lance found that the more often students received instruction from the library media specialist, the higher the test scores. Successful and thriving library media programs have library media specialists who spend the majority of their time working with students. The Ohio Study by Dr. Ross Todd, Dr. Carol Kuhlthau, and OELMA showed that an effective school library, led by a credentialed library media specialist, plays a critical role in facilitating student learning for building knowledge.

Read the guidelines in *Information Power* and look at the roles of the library media specialist: program administrator, instructional partner, and information specialist, and teacher. All of them are important, but the library media specialist's role in instruction in collaboration with teachers is where the library media specialist has the biggest opportunity to impact student achievement.

For example at a recent workshop, a classroom teacher said, "Our library media specialist just reads a story and then the kids check out books." While just reading stories is great because it exposes students to books that are above their reading level and helps with vocabulary development, the library media specialist is missing an opportunity to expand on that read-aloud experience. During story time, the library media specialist can ask questions for:

- Comprehension
  - What do you think this word means? Why?
  - What was the problem in the story? How did the main character solve it?
  - What do you think the author was trying to say in this book?
- Prediction
  - What do you think will happen next?
  - What can we guess will happen based on the cover? The pictures?
  - Now that the story is over, what do you think might happen to these characters next?
- Summarization
  - What happened in the first, middle, end of the story?
  - Put in order the events that happened in the story. What happened first, second, third, etc.?
  - Why do you think the characters acted the way they did?

Stories with patterns or repeating phrases can provide students an opportunity to read with the library media specialist and work on fluency. Another learning opportunity in storytime is to talk about genres such as poetry, historical fiction, folk tales, fairy tales, etc. Students should be exposed to all types of literature and given strategies for reading and comprehending them.

Another way to include instruction in story time is to include non-fiction as well as fiction. Biographies, autobiographies, and other types of informational text should be shared with students. Asking questions to help the students find, use, and evaluate information in the books being read aloud to them is an additional technique to use. While using informational text, students are learning decoding, comprehension, and analysis skills. These ideas turn a simple read-aloud into an opportunity for instruction.

In secondary education, nearly the entire focus of reading in the content areas is in informational text. Students will need a variety of strategies for breaking down what can be difficult reading into smaller parts that they can understand (Gambrell, Morrow, and Pressley, 128).

KNOW THE SCHOOL'S READING PHILOSOPHY

The library media specialist should be keenly aware of how reading is taught in the building. Some questions library media specialists might ask about teaching reading in their schools might be:

- Is it a balanced-literacy approach – guided reading (whole group and leveled groups), sustained silent reading, writing, and word building?
- Is there more of an emphasis on phonics? Comprehension?
- Is there a specific reading program such as Four Blocks™ (guided reading, word building, sustained silent reading, and writing) or Road to the Code™ (phonological awareness program) being used in the building?
- Are there certain skills that classroom teachers focus on at certain times of the year? What are the major skills teachers work on with students the entire year?
- Are basal text used exclusively, in conjunction with trade books, or are trade books used exclusively?
- Do the teachers use leveled texts? How?

Answers to these questions cause the library media specialist to begin to think about the ways the library media program is supporting teaching:

- Does the library media program offer extended hours? Summer hours?
- Does the library media program provide resources for parents?
- What are the check-out policies? Do they foster a love of reading?
- Does the collection provide resources for supporting the teaching of reading? Are there materials for all types of readers (emergent, struggling, high ability)?
- Do students have consistent and flexible access to the library media center?
- What role does the library media specialist play in teaching reading?
- How does reading instruction impact research skills?
- How can the library media specialist integrate technology to help teach reading?

Library media specialists constantly share with students the importance of information and the fact that information can be a powerful tool. Knowing what is happening in the classroom is important no matter what kind of schedule the library media program operates. On a fixed schedule when each class has a set time each week to work with the library media specialist and the teacher typically does not remain in the room, curriculum knowledge provides the library media specialist an opportunity to align the media center lessons, units, and projects with the classroom collection. In a flexible schedule where instruction is scheduled at the point of need and the teacher remains with the students and is actively involved in instruction, the library media specialist and classroom teacher plan, teach, and assess together. Classroom teachers are going to be more inclined to work with someone who understands what they are doing and who indicates a willingness to help them.

Research shows that flexible scheduling continues to be the ideal method of instruction in the library media center. Dr. Keith Curry Lance and his co-researchers found in Illinois that students who had more flexible access to the library media center had higher scores on the state assessment. Brain research by Dr. Pat Wolfe and others tells us that students need to make connections with what they are learning and not be taught skills in isolation. When information literacy skills are embedded into the classroom curriculum and not in an isolated library setting, students will retain more information literacy skills.

GATHERING INFORMATION

★ *As library media specialists are learning how reading is taught in school, they are going to amass a great deal of information. In Chapter 2, it was suggested to create a binder with all the state standards for easy reference. One suggestion is to expand that binder to include copies of curriculum, yearlong plans, scope and sequences, etc. All the information that can be found about what is being taught in the school should be located in one place for easy access. Taking it a step further, color-coding these yearlong plans by grade level or department makes it easy to flip to the correct one while planning with teachers. Depending on the size of the school, more than one binder may be necessary. Having the information organized in advance can help the library media specialist see where connections can be made to information literacy skills. In addition, ideas will be generated for opportunities to work together on projects that will help the school meet the school improvement goals.*

Another tool the library media specialist should want to have available to them is copies of the teachers' manuals for textbooks. Ask the curriculum director to order an extra set of the teachers' manuals. This is a good idea for each subject – not just reading. At first this may seem like an odd request since library media specialists are not involved in daily teaching of the subject; however, knowing what stories are being read, what skills are stressed, and what teachers are using can help the library media specialist in planning with teachers. If it is not possible to get copies of the teachers' manuals for the library media specialist, at least take time to get familiar with the books. Having access and knowledge of all the instructional tools available in the school opens the door to collaboration and planning.

LOVE OF READING

The instructional role for library media specialists goes beyond being part of helping students learn how to read. It is important that students also learn to love to read and want to read. Some of the reason include:

- Employment
- Entertainment
- Personal information
- Direction following
- Civic awareness

Library media specialists can match readers to books helping to foster that love of reading. They can introduce students to new authors, new titles, and books on topics they are interested in reading. Collaborative projects that include author and illustrator studies are a great way to introduce students to the vast amount of literature available. Booktalks introduce students to new books and authors. Reader's Advisory Groups allow for feedback from the students to the library media specialist on what they want to read.

⭐ *Students need to see library media specialists, teachers, and adults who love to read and share that joy with their students. One idea is to put a poster up in the library media center highlighting what children's books you are currently reading. The library media specialist can add titles as the year progresses to create a list of books they read.*

There is not going to be one thing that motivates all students – one thing that works for Johnny may not interest Susie at all, so it is a big undertaking. However, individualization not only can show students that they are important but also that reading is important, too. Reading can be a social event as well. Set up a book club where students come and share and talk about what they are reading.

ADOLESCENT LITERACY

Literacy instruction at the secondary level focuses heavily within content areas. If students are unable to read content materials, they will be unable to learn about or research the topics. It is important to look at how our middle and high schools can help those students who are still struggling and help higher achieving students get even better.

Reading at the secondary level can provide a perfect opportunity for a library media specialist to help. Cris Tovani shares in her book *Do I Really Have to Teach Reading?* that specific content areas require specific skills for reading and understanding. Students will need different reading strategies for reading a science textbook as opposed to building plans in a industrial technology course. She advises teachers to take time to model these strategies with their students prior to assigning the content-rich text so that students can be more successful.

Many secondary teachers were never trained in teaching reading. They have a fountain of knowledge about their content, but they don't know how to break it down for those students who need additional help with the text. Tovani talks about teachers slowing down and thinking about how they digest the materials. Consider what they are doing while reading, such as figuring out vocabulary in context, looking to see if the author is a valid authority, etc, and then share those with their students.

As schools continue to stress literacy and test scores, content area teachers will continue to have pressure to help teach students to read. Library media specialists can use that as an opportunity for collaboration. With access to a plethora of resources, teaching skills, and information literacy processes, library media specialists are poised to help lead the way with teaching reading in the school.

COLLABORATION

As library media specialists assist with research, they can provide strategies for understanding the material. They can help find materials at a variety of reading levels. Also, they can offer to help teachers learn techniques for working with struggling readers. By working collaboratively, the adult-to-students ratio decreases – a classroom teacher and a library media specialist to 30 students as opposed to one teacher to 30. Team-teaching allows more time to focus on individual students who need additional help.

WRITING

Teaching students to write can be an important part of the library media specialist's contribution. A wealth of good writing lies at the library media specialist's finger tips on the shelves of a library media center. A library media specialist can use these great works to inspire students to want to write and can find examples and qualities that exemplify good writing. It is very common to teach writing in "mini-lessons" focused on a specific skill students need to develop in their writing. Library media specialists and classroom teachers can plan together and find opportunities for the library media specialist to teach some of those mini-lessons.

SPECIAL INTEREST GROUPS

Collaborating with special education teachers can be a fabulous connection for students. Often the teachers attempt to cover the same content but have to modify the amount and level of the materials. The library media specialist and the special education teacher can plan research projects and gear the topics and projects to the students. The library media specialist can also find reading materials that can be used by the special education student or English language learner. They can continue to learn the same topics and themes the classroom teacher is covering, but more on a level they can understand.

STRATEGIES

Based on the definition of literacy for this book, the following examples illustrate how library media specialists can impact this area of instruction. It is not meant to be an all-inclusive list but rather some ideas to get the mind working so that library media specialists can tailor these and/or create their own ideas to their specific buildings.

ALPHABETICS: PHONEMIC AWARENESS AND PHONICS

> *Lisa Hunt, a library media specialist from Moore, Oklahoma, uses poetry with her students to work on sounds and letters. She puts the poetry up on the wall and students look for letters, sounds, rhyming words, etc. as they read and re-read the poem.*

Take students on a sound hunt. For example, let's say students were working on the sounds for letter *s*. Where are all the places in the library media center that have an /s/ sound in them? Where do students see the letter *s* written? Take digital cameras so that students can take pictures of all the *s* words they might find. This might be an activity that the library media specialist does with a small group of students – rotating groups until all students have gotten a chance to participate.

Use the letter as a scavenger hunt in the library. Can students find things that start with the /m/ sound in the library, like magazines or movies? Can students find the same sound as /ch/, such as check-out desk, children's books, or chapter books?

Do this same activity with any story that the library media specialist might be sharing with a class. Can students find the sounds and the letters that make those sounds in the story?

One use of technology is to use the resources found on subscription video streaming services. Videos from online sources such as Discovery Education Streaming, <http://streaming.discoveryeducation.com>, or Safari Montage™, <www.safarimontage.com>, have several small video clips that could be used as a learning station for students.

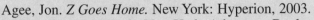

PHONICS AND PHONEMIC AWARENESS BIBLIOGRAPHY

Agee, Jon. *Z Goes Home*. New York: Hyperion, 2003.

Cronin, Doreen. *Wiggle*. New York: Atheneum Books for Young Readers, 2005.

Fisher, Valorie. *Ellsworth's Extraordinary Electric Ears and Other Amazing Alphabet Anecdotes*. New York: Atheneum Books for Young Readers, 2003.

Foster, John. *Barron's Junior Rhyming Dictionary*. Hauppauge, N.Y: Barron's Educational Series, 2006.

Glaser, Milton, and Shirley Glaser. *The Alphazeds*. New York: Miramax Books, 2003.

Heling, Kathryn, and Deborah Hembrook. *Mouse Makes Words: A Phonics Reader*. New York: Random House, 2002.

Martin, Bill, and John Archambault. *Chicka Chicka Boom Boom*. New York: Simon & Schuster Books for Young Readers, 1989.

Sierra, Judy. *Schoolyard Rhymes: Kids' Own Rhymes for Rope Skipping, Hand Clapping, Ball Bouncing, and Just Plain Fun*. New York: A. Knopf, 2005.

Stamper, Judith B., and Wiley Blevins. *Boom! Zoom!* New York: Scholastic Inc, 1997.

Stamper, Judith B., and Wiley Blevins. *Monster Town*. New York: Scholastic Inc., 1997.

Stamper, Judith B., and Wiley Blevins. *Monster Town Fair*. New York: Scholastic, 1998.

Turner, Priscilla. *The War Between the Vowels and the Consonants*. New York: Farrar, Straus and Giroux, 1996.

Wood, Audrey. *Alphabet Adventure*. New York: Blue Sky Press, 2001.

FLUENCY

Fluency is where the heart of reading and library media programs go hand-in-hand. For students to become better readers, they need the opportunity to practice reading aloud. In searching for ideas to support this in the library media center, a place to start might be library media policies.

- How long can students keep materials?
- How many items can they borrow?
- Can they renew them?
- Is that a sufficient time for them to have a chance to re-read and share with adults?
- Are they limited to only books they can read?

- Is there a way to set up a system in which volunteers, parents, or other staff members in the building can listen to students reading the books they have borrowed from the media center?
- Can you create an incentive program for students who read their library books to their parents when they check them out?
- Are there materials available at a variety of reading levels and a variety of topics?
- Are there other formats for materials, such as comic books, magazines, and graphic novels?

While the concept has been around for quite a while, in recent years Readers Theatre has become popular as a major strategy for practicing fluency. Several books and magazines publish pre-written scripts for student use (see Figure 3.1 for a Readers Theatre Bibliography). Reading aloud provides students an opportunity to read with expression and emotion, which in

RESOURCES FOR READERS THEATRE

Online:
Aaron Shepard's Readers Theatre -
   <www.aaronshep.com/rt/index.html>

Magazines:
Library Sparks Magazines, published by Highsmith has a monthly Readers Theatre script by author Toni Buzzeo.

Books:
Gustafson, Chris. *Acting Out*. Worthington, OH: Linworth Publishing, 2002.

Gustafson, Chris. *Acting Cool! Using Reader's Theatre to Teach Language Arts and Social Studies in Your Classroom*. Worthington, OH: Linworth Publishing, 2003.

Gustafson, Chris. *Acting Cool! Using Reader's Theatre to Teach Math and Science in Your Classroom*. Worthington, OH: Linworth Publishing, 2003.

Lombardo, Mary A. *Rhymes, Writing, and Role-Play*, Worthington, OH: Linworth Publishing, 2004.

Readers Theatre Series, Westport, CT: Libaries Unlimited, 1989-2007.

Leveled Readers Theatre Scripts:
Benchmark Education
   <www.benchmarkeducation.com>
Reading AtoZ
   <www.readingatoz.com>

Figure 3.1

turn helps develop fluency. It also helps to build a student's confidence. Some companies are even providing scripts at various reading levels or with each character at a different level, so an entire class can work on fluency together while each student can read and work with text that is at their level.

Morning announcements are also a great way for students to practice reading aloud. The script pattern and format are often consistent from day to day allowing students the opportunity to practice emotion and inflection when they read. Students can also present their Readers Theatre plays on the morning announcement show. As they practice their scripts and begin to improve, they use their morning announcement show as a showcase for the students to share their readings with the entire school.

Booktalk books in a series are also a good way to help students work on their fluency. Because books written in a series are typically at about the same reading level and follow the same writing structure and pattern, students can become better readers as they work their way through the series. Students flock to series like *Junie B. Jones* or *Magic Tree House Tales*, but the library media specialist can help them find other series like the *Cody* books by Betsy Duffey or *Owen Foote* series by Stephanie Greene.

FLUENCY BIBLIOGRAPHY*

Butler, Dori, and Frank Sofo. *The Time Capsule*. Pelham, NY: Benchmark Education Co., 2005.

Fuerst, Jeffrey B., and Anita DuFalla. *How the Hubba-Dubbas Saved Lake Ni-Ni*. Pelham, NY: Benchmark Education Co., 2004.

Hoberman, Mary A. *You Read to Me, I'll Read to You: Very Short Fairy Tales to Read Together*. New York: Little, Brown and Company, 2004.

Hoberman, Mary A. *You Read to Me, I'll Read to You: Very Short Mother Goose Tales to Read Together*. New York: Little, Brown and Company, 2005.

Hoberman, Mary A. *You Read to Me, I'll Read to You: Very Short Stories to Read Together*. Boston: Little, Brown and Company, 2001.

Kramer, Candice. *Ben Franklin's Visit: A When Machine Play*. Pelham, NY: Benchmark Education Co., 2003.

Sierra, Judy. *Schoolyard Rhymes: Kids' Own Rhymes for Rope Skipping, Hand Clapping, Ball Bouncing, and Just Plain Fun*. New York: A. Knopf, 2005.

* Note: Almost any book will work for fluency. The key is to read and re-read it so that as you build confidence in reading the passage you can spend more time on comprehension and reading with emotion.

COMPREHENSION: VOCABULARY INSTRUCTION

⭐ *The most logical connection between resources in the library media center and teaching vocabulary is the dictionary. For younger grades, students can find the glossary at the back of the book in series such as Rookie Readers™ by Scholastic Library Publishing, Fast Fact™ books by Capstone, or Weekly Reader™ books by Gareth Stevens Publishing. Students will begin to make the connection of, "When I find a word I don't know, I can look it up to find the meaning." Older students can move on to dictionaries and thesauruses for help with vocabulary words. Tie these activities into subjects in the classroom. If the students are working on wolves and habitats then use the words and vocabulary association with those themes when teaching students how to use the dictionary or thesaurus.*

Tools such as the online Merriam-Webster dictionary, <www.merriamwebster.com>, or the subscription based Visual Thesaurus, <www.visualthesaurus.com>, provide electronic sources for students to use when looking up unfamiliar words. One activity is to take a book like *A Splendid Friend Indeed* by Suzanne Bloom and have students find words that are similar in meaning to replace the words in the title. If students replaced those words throughout the book would it still make sense?

For a project on a grander scale, GeorgeAnne Draper, library media specialist at Wynne High School in Wynne, Arkansas, worked with her school to create an all-school reading event. To help support an author visit, each student received a copy of the author's book, and the entire building read the book together. To help with comprehension of the book and to teach vocabulary, each day a word was chosen from the book and a mini-lesson was taught in each first period classroom. On the announcements, the word was used during the script and students were able to enter a contest if they could correctly write down the new vocabulary word used on the news – stressing their listening comprehension skills. The library media program worked to help implement the school-wide reading program, one of the strategies listed in their school improvement plan to help students improve reading, reading comprehension, and writing skills.

COMPREHENSION: VOCABULARY INSTRUCTION BIBLIOGRAPHY

Banks, Kate. *Max's Words.* New York: Farrar, Straus and Giroux, 2006.

Cassie, Brian. *Say It Again.* Watertown, MA: Charlesbridge, 2000.

Clements, Andrew. *Double Trouble in Walla Walla.* Brookfield, CT: Millbrook Press, 1997.

Filipek, Nina, and Jan Smith. *Early Words.* Kettering Northamptonshire, UK: Book Studio, 2006.

Frasier, Debra. *Miss Alaineus: A Vocabulary Disaster.* San Diego, CA.: Harcourt, Inc., 2000.

Hook, J.N. *The Grand Panjandrum and 2,699 Other Rare, Useful, and Delightful Words and Expressions.* New York: Collier Books, 1991.

Hopkins, Lee B. *Wonderful Words: Poems About Reading, Writing, Speaking, and Listening.* New York: Simon & Schuster Books for Young Readers, 2004.

Howe, Randy. *Word Source: The Smarter Way to Learn Vocabulary Words.* New York: Simon & Schuster, 2005.

Ostler, Rosemarie. *Dewdroppers, Waldos, and Slackers: A Decade-by-Decade Guide to the Vanishing Vocabulary of the Twentieth Century.* Oxford, Eng.: Oxford University Press, 2003.

Schotter, Roni. *The Boy Who Loved Words.* New York: Schwartz & Wade Books, 2006.

Shulman, Mark. *Mom and Dad Are Palindromes: A Dilemma for Words . . . and Backwards.* San Francisco: Chronicle Books, 2006.

Thomson, Ruth. *A First Thesaurus.* North Mankato, MN: Thameside Press, 2002.

Thomson, Ruth. *A First Word Bank.* North Mankato, MN: Thameside Press, 2002.

Umstatter, Jack. *Where Words Come From.* New York: F. Watts, 2002.

COMPREHENSION: TEXT COMPREHENSION

⭐ *Providing students with that "just right book" has always been one of the valued roles of a library media specialist. Those "just right books" not only are ones that students want to read but also ones which they will be successful in building their reading skills and knowledge. Share with students the five-finger test of reading a page. If he or she finds more than five difficult words on a page, then likely that book may be too difficult for them. There are systems that will match library materials with reading levels such as Lexiles® or Accelerated Reader® levels. Library media specialists who work closely with teachers can help guide students during book selection for those "just right books" because they are more familiar with the strengths and weaknesses of each child.*

However, these leveling programs should not be the only factor for students choosing library materials to check out. Working with teachers, the library media specialist can help to provide free choice as well so that students are picking the materials they want to read. For example, the check-out policy may be that students must have at least one "just right" book and several others of their own choice. Choices should not be solely limited to certain sections or levels. There are wonderful non-fiction resources for students, but if kindergarteners are limited to just picture books, they will never discover them. It is a fine line, but library media specialists can help keep it balanced.

Beyond helping students select just the right book, library media specialists can help with comprehension as they work with classroom teachers to design research projects. Library media specialists work to find resources at a variety of reading levels to meet the variety of reading needs of the students. By working with classroom teachers to identify those students who need extra help or a different text, library media specialists can teach students how to find resources where they can be successful.

Book clubs are also a way to build comprehension while students discuss books they have read. These can be part of classroom study, an after school-club, a family book club in collaboration with the PTA/PTO, or even a lunch-bunch group. By focusing on certain topics, authors, or even a particular book, the discussion allows students to think about what they read and build a deeper knowledge. Besides providing a source for the books, library media specialists can help organize these clubs and be part of the discussion with the students. The students become a great reader's advisory group, too, by giving input and suggestions on what types of materials they would like to see in the library media center.

COMPREHENSION: TEXT COMPREHENSION BIBLIOGRAPHY*

For topics on a variety of levels, start with some
of these publishers:

- Gareth Stevens
  <www.garethstevens.com>
- Capstone Press
  <www.capstonepress.com>
- Scholastic Library Publishing
  <http://librarypublishing.scholastic.com>

Harris, Raymond. *Best Short Stories. Middle Level: 10 Stories for Young Adults with Lessons for Teaching the Basic Elements of Literature.* Lincolnwood, IL: Jamestown Publishers, 1998.

Warrick, Karen C., and Becky Radtke. *Story Elements: Learning About the Components of Stories to Deepen Comprehension.* Grand Rapids, MI: Instructional Fair/TSDenison, 2001.

* Note: Most books lend themselves to developing comprehension questions. Keep in mind they should be more than just recall questions; they should also get the reader thinking about what they read and try to help them make connections.

FREE VOLUNTARY READING

Perhaps one of the easiest ways a library media specialist can be a part of school improvement literacy goals is in Free Voluntary Reading (FVR). Many library media specialists have worked with their administrators and teachers to set up free voluntary reading times in their schools. They provide resources for reading during that time and model reading themselves during those FVR moments (Krashen).

Benita Brown of Sacajawea Elementary in Richland, Washington, promotes reading by encouraging her students to read during the summer. She helps students get library cards at the public library, provides information to parents about programs such as the public library's summer reading program, and links online to the public library from the school library Web page. She communicates the importance and love of reading through all these vehicles while increasing the knowledge about opportunities for reading beyond just the school.

ADOLESCENT READING

★ *To help their students read more, Matoaca High School in Chesterfield, Virginia, set up a summer reading program for all grade levels. The library media specialist, Alda Moore, was an active part of that process. She was a member of the title selection committee and provided copies of those books in the library media center. Their library media center checks out books that students may keep over the summer and Moore contacts the local bookstores and public libraries to let them know what titles are on the list that summer, so they can stock up on them. To expand on this idea, the library media specialist could set up a blog or Wiki where students could share about the books they are reading all summer long. Students could also have a formal book discussion on the titles during the first few days of school.*

At the secondary level, a library media specialist's role as a resource locator can be useful in content areas such as science or social studies. Teachers in these areas may have students who are not able to read the required text. Beyond the general education student, there are many subgroups such as special education and English Language Learners that also will require a variety of reading levels. Library media specialists can help them find texts, articles, and audio books that these students can use successfully.

Collaboration with the teacher is key to having time to search for resources on a variety of reading levels. Statewide databases, inter-library loan requests from public and academic librarians, and research in the library media center resources takes time. The more planning done ahead of time, the more success students can have when the library media specialist and classroom teacher can direct them to the resources that best fit their needs.

WRITING

⭐ *Writing, just like research, is a process. Just as schools have adopted a research process/model, so too schools have begun to use a common vocabulary for the writing process. As library media specialists work with students, it is important to use that same vernacular used in the classroom. Many of the information-literacy skills easily weave in and out of the writing process. For example, the first step in writing is to prewrite, when students are jotting down ideas and thoughts about what they are going to write about. Sometimes those ideas require research of information. Students need to know more about a topic before they can determine if they want to write about it. This provides some connection between writing and information literacy.*

Gwen Tetrick, library media specialist at Stony Creek Elementary School in Noblesville, Indiana, uses students' writer's notebooks to expand on activities in the library media center. Students write responses to literature, original pieces, and notes for their projects. All of this is kept in their writer's notebook in the library media center for easy use and organization. The notebook is an easy way for students to be organized about the stage in the writing process they are in and the next step they are ready to start. The notebook could also be a good place to save bibliographies, book lists, online database information, etc.

Writing also provides an excellent opportunity to expand on ethical use of information and the appropriate way to cite sources and use information garnered from research. Library media specialists can also help develop fiction writers by promoting good writing found on the shelves of the library media center, providing a forum for students to share their writing, and by providing resources in the collection to help students become better writers.

Library media collections are full of great writers. Harvest some of the best and share those with students as models of good writing. For example, Richard Peck's first lines are always amazing and quick to grab the reader into the story. Read to the students the opening line from *The Teacher's Funeral,* and they will be clamoring to read the rest of the book. Library media specialists and teachers want students to think that same way when they write. What will make people want to read my writing?

Use the library media center as a place for students to share their writing. Post student writing up in the library media center. Allow students to donate their writing to the library media center collection and circulate it to other students. Post it on the library media center Web page, with parental consent. Have a reading event where students who want to share their writing can read it aloud to others. All writers need an audience, so the library media center can provide them with a variety of forums for sharing their writing.

It might seem obvious, but the library media center must make available resources for writers. Create a writer center where paper, pencils, erasers, computers, etc. are all easily accessible. Make sure to include dictionaries and thesauruses – print, online, or both. Author J.K. Rowling, when she first started, would write in a cafe in England. Perhaps the next great writers will find the library media center the perfect place for them to write.

WRITING BIBLIOGRAPHY

Fletcher, Ralph J. *A Writer's Notebook: Unlocking the Writer Within You.* New York: Avon Books, 1996.

Fletcher, Ralph J. *How Writers Work: Finding a Process that Works for You.* New York: HarperTrophy, 2000.

Fletcher, Ralph J. *Live Writing: Breathing Life into Your Words.* New York: Avon Books, 1999.

Hopkins, Lee B. *Wonderful Words: Poems About Reading, Writing, Speaking, and Listening.* New York: Simon & Schuster Books for Young Readers, 2004.

Kehret, Peg. *Five Pages a Day: A Writer's Journey.* Morton Grove, IL: A. Whitman, 2002.

King, Penny, and Ruth Thomson. *Start Writing About People and Places.* North Mankato, MN: Thameside Press, 2001.

King, Penny, and Ruth Thomson. *Start Writing About Things I Do.* North Mankato, MN: Thameside Press, 2001.

King, Penny, and Ruth Thomson. *Start Writing Adventure Stories.* North Mankato, MN: Thameside Press, 2001.

Leedy, Loreen. *Look at My Book: How Kids Can Write & Illustrate Terrific Books.* New York: Holiday House, 2004.

McNaughton, Colin. *Once Upon an Ordinary School Day.* New York: Farrar Straus Giroux, 2005.

Nobisso, Josephine. *Josephine Nobisso's Show; Don't Tell!: Secrets of Writing.* Westhampton Beach, N.Y: Gingerbread House, 2004.

Olien, Rebecca. *Kids Write!:Fantasy & Sci Fi, Mystery, Autobiography, Adventure & More!* Nashville, TN: Williamson Books, 2005.

Park, Linda S. *Project Mulberry.* New York: Clarion, 2005.

Peck, Richard. *Invitations to the World: Teaching and Writing for Young.* New York: Dial Books, 2002.

Rhatigan, Joe. *In Print!: 40 Cool Publishing Projects for Kids.* New York: Lark Books, 2003.

Thomson, Ruth. *A First Thesaurus.* North Mankato, MN: Thameside Press, 2002.

Thomson, Ruth. *A First Word Bank.* North Mankato, MN: Thameside Press, 2002.

Thomson, Ruth. *Go Further with Grammar: Exclamations Are Expressive!: Adverbs Add Extra Impact.* North Mankato, MN: Thameside Press, 2002.

Thomson, Ruth. *Grammar Is Great! Verbs Are Vital! Connectives Connect.* North Mankato, MN: Thameside Press, 2002.

Thomson, Ruth. *Start Writing Amazing Stories.* North Mankato, MN: Thameside Press, 2001.

RESEARCH PROCESS

Literacy seems the logical place to think about research in terms of the school improvement process. There are a variety of research models out there. As the amount of information continues to grow at a rapid rate, it will be impossible for schools to cover all the content students may need to know. Library media specialists can use this as an opportunity, as the school improvement plans are written, or revised, to adopt a model to use throughout the building or district.

Indiana has recently even added research directly into the English/ Language Arts Standards when they were revised in 2006. According to these standards, students in grades 2 through 12 should complete a project that uses a systematic research process. A standard like that is a perfect opening to collaborating with teachers because now students must be given that experience.

⭐ *Adopting a model is only the beginning. Implementing the model to help students will be the important hurdle to jump. At one elementary school, they adopted the Big6™ by Michael Eisenberg and Robert Berkowitz. The library media specialist worked with teachers to develop a research journal that would help students go through the process on every project. Teachers in second through fourth grade agreed to use this format for all research projects. Following that, posters were purchased for each room and the library media center so that students saw that the Big6™ was more than something they just used in the library.*

As students are learning strategies for working with informational text, for example, the research in the library media center becomes a perfect opportunity for them to apply those skills. The library media specialist and classroom teacher will be able to move around and help students one-on-one. When they notice several students struggle with the same type of text or resource, it could be useful to do a mini-lesson for the entire class on how to get the most from that source of information.

COPYRIGHT AND PLAGIARISM

As part of the research process, it is important for students to learn to properly cite their sources. From the first research project a student does, he or she must begin to learn about copyright and plagiarism. With young researchers, library media specialists can talk about using the students' own words when writing down facts. It is quickly apparent which students are struggling with research or the source they are using because they will copy sources verbatim. When the teacher or library media specialist asks them to tell them what they wrote, they can read the words but not tell what they mean. Writing a summary of what you read is a good strategy for reading comprehension and that aligns well with taking notes for research. This provides a perfect opportunity for the library media specialist to talk about plagiarism, work with the student one-on-one while they use that resource, and/or direct them to another source where they may be more successful.

COLLECTION DEVELOPMENT

Library media specialists try to select materials on a variety of reading levels that are rich in content and information and that appeal to readers – getting all of that on a finite amount of money. In addition, library media specialists need to be attentive to recreational reading. Knowledge of what their students are reading is critical. Are students reading: Magazines? Graphic Novels? Fiction? Non-Fiction? The collection should be diverse and offer readers materials they want to read (see Figure 3.2 for Collection Development Resources).

Sondra Patchett, library media specialist at Kankakee High School in Kankakee, Illinois, had no graphic novels in her collection, but some of the students and teachers were starting to ask for them. She asked for volunteer students to review some graphic novels and share these reviews with her. The response was overwhelming, and she and the students have decided together what to purchase. Steven Krashen says in *The Power of Reading* that it doesn't matter what people read as long as they are reading. If library media specialists provide resources and materials that students will read, that will help make them better readers.

COLLECTION DEVELOPMENT RESOURCES

Association for Library Service to Children Book Awards
   **<www.ala.org/ala/alsc/awardsscholarships/literacyawds/
   literacyrelated.cfm>**
Association for Library Service to Children Resources
   <www.ala.org/ala/alsc/alscresources/resources.cfm>
Association for Library Service to Children Children's Notables Lists
   **<www.ala.org/ala/alsc/awardsscholarships/childrensnotable/
   default.cfm>**
Young Adult Library Services Association Booklists & Book Awards
   <www.ala.org/YALSATemplate.cfm?Section=booklistsawards>
Outstanding Science Trade Books
   <www.nsta.org/publications/ostb/>
National Council for the Social Studies – Notable Trade Book for Young
   People
   <www.socialstudies.org/resources/notable/>
State Student Choice Book Awards – compilation by Sharon McElmeel
   <www.mcelmeel.com/curriculum/bookawards.html>

Figure 3.2

The library media center collection should be a vital resource for
teachers and students.

- Does it contain materials that teachers can use when they need to
  demonstrate effective use of figurative language?
- Are there books that model writing, such as good beginnings, good
  endings, or setting up a climax in a story?
- Are collections of books that demonstrate a plot with a climax available?
- Are there resources for English language learners or special education students?

Library media specialists need to be aware of what skills are being
taught so they can provide materials and resources to support instruction.
Standards, yearlong plans, and textbooks all are good places to start for this
information. Many textbooks also provide lists of trade books that will sup-
plement a unit or story in the textbook. Review the list and purchase those
materials that will be useful to staff and students. Interlibrary loans and bor-
rowing from the public library provide other sources for materials when the
library media center collection may not have the resources or the funds to
purchase everything needed.

LEVELED LIBRARY BRANCH
A SERVICE OF YOUR LIBRARY MEDIA CENTER

Purpose
The mission of the Leveled Library Branch is to provide a one-stop clearinghouse of leveled reader materials at North Elementary School for use with Guided Reading.

Leveling System
Fountas and Pinnell® (Others to choose from include Reading Recovery®, Lexiles®, etc.)

Set-up
- The Leveled Library located in old conference room.
- Access 24/7 provides for teachers.
- The level system is only for items in the Leveled Library Branch.
- A Computer with the automation system will be set-up in the Leveled Library Branch for teachers to search the collection and check items out.
- Items will be cataloged so that searching can be done by title, author, level, and subject.
- Books are shelved by levels, then by Dewey Decimal System.
- Each set will contain approximately 5 to 7 copies of the same title.
- Each set will be kept in a plastic bag, and the barcode for checking out will be located on the bag.
- Each bag will be bar-coded and labeled with title, author, level, and number of copies.
- Each will be designated with the circulation type of "Leveled Sets".
- Each book will be stamped that it is a "Leveled Library Branch Book"
- Call Number Prefix – LSx where x = the level of the book.
  - Example: Shelia the Brave by Kevin Henkes
  - LSK HEN

Process for Circulation
- Teachers come to the Leveled Library and select the books they wish to check out.
- Books check out as complete sets (even if the teacher needs just one or two copies, the entire bag must be checked out!)

Figure 3.3

- Books will check out for two weeks.
- Teachers will use automation system to check out leveled sets to their name.
- Teachers will return the leveled sets when they are finished to the Library Media Center.
- A library media assistant will check materials in and re-shelve them in the Leveled Library.

Process of Adding New Titles
- New titles will be added when funding is available from grants, PTO, and/or the principal.
- The book budget for the library media center will remain for the main library media center and not used for the Leveled Library.
- To obtain level of the new titles:
    - check Fountas and Pinnell books or check <www.FountasandPinnellleveledbooks.com>
- Ask Title 1 staff to level text.
- Items are cataloged and processed for the shelves.

Figure 3.3 continued

Vendors like Baker and Taylor™, Bound to Stay Bound™, and Follett Library Resource™ all have online assessments that will rate the library media collection. These analyses can provide data to help when advocating for more funds. If the school improvement goal is math and the math section in the library media center is extremely out of date, then the library media specialist needs to use the data to advocate for funds to update that area.

LEVELED TEXTS

Leveled texts are becoming increasingly more widespread in schools. There are a variety of leveling systems such as Fountas and Pinnell®, Reading Recovery®, DRA®, Lexiles®, etc. Unfortunately, many library media specialists have heard horror stories of administrators and teachers wanting to reorganize the library media collection based on reading levels. One option is to offer a leveled library as part of the library media program.

Leveled libraries typically consist of 3-6 copies of a title bundled together for teachers to check out for use with small groups. In these small groups, students are working with text that is at their instructional level. The books should be stored separately from the main library collection. For example at one elementary, they are housed in an old conference room down the hall referred to fondly as the "Leveled Library: A Branch of the Library Media Center." These resources can be cataloged into the automation system. A computer is setup in the room so that teachers can check them out right there. The library media specialist can provide data to administrators about how often books are used and keep track of them. Many of these rooms are huge investments, so keeping track of those resources cuts down on the numbers that go missing. It demonstrates how the library media specialist is providing a leveled collection for teachers to use in instruction, while at the same time leaving the library media center's regular collection unleveled for free choice. Teachers use the books at school and sometimes send them home with students as well. Reading A to Z, <www.readingAtoZ.com>, is an online source of printable leveled books, and often these are sent home because they are easy to make more of them. The leveled library needs more than just primary, beginning reading books; it also should contain a variety of books at all levels. Teachers of third and fourth grade may want more chapter books and higher level informational text than primary teachers, so it is important the library offers a variety.

At the secondary level, considerations of reading level and comprehension are important. Are there a variety of materials at a variety of reading levels for students? Can students who are struggling find materials to help them research and understand the topic? Are there support resources such as dictionaries for specific content areas that may help students who

SOURCES FOR LEVELED BOOKS

Benchmark Books
>   **<www.benchmarkeducation.com>**
Reading A to Z
>   **<www.readingatoz.com>**
Rigby
>   **<http://rigby.harcourtachieve.com>**
Scholastic
>   **<www.scholastic.com>**
Wright Group
>   **<www.wrightgroup.com>**

are struggling with the content vocabulary? Does the fiction section contain a variety of reading levels? Are there special collections, such as graphic novels that might appeal to reluctant readers and other readers?

Finally, remember that a professional collection is also a way to provide resources that the school improvement committee and other teachers in the building can use when looking for strategies and ideas. Books and periodicals that provide professional resources are important for library media specialists to consider. Look for resources that provide support to the school improvement plan. A variety of books on the same topic can provide a wealth of ideas and allow the school improvement committee to make informed decisions on what strategies to implement.

REFLECTION

Today's students need to be good readers and writers as they enter the work force. The subject of literacy aligns to the most "traditional" role of the library media specialist and library media center. Library media specialists are moving beyond the traditional role of providing books and materials to students and teachers. Successful library media specialists must also be part of the instructional team that helps teach students how to read and write and therefore help students meet the goals outlined in the school improvement plan.

PROFESSIONAL RESOURCES

Allington, Richard. *What Really Matters for Struggling Readers*. Boston: Pearson/Allyn and Bacon, 2006.

Bush, Gail. *Every Student Reads*. Chicago: American Library Association, 2005.

Callison, Daniel, and Leslie B. Preddy. *The Blue Book on Information Age Inquiry, Instruction and Literacy*. Littleton, CO: Libraries Unlimited, 2006.

Cox, Marge, Carl A. Harvey II, and Susan E. Page. *The Library Media Specialist and the Writing Process*. Worthington, OH: Linworth Publishing, Inc., 2007.

Everhart, Nancy, and Nancy McGriff. "Long-Term Tracking of Student Participants' Reading Achievement in Reading Motivation Programs." *Knowledge Quest* May/June 2002: 43-46.

Fountas, Irene, and Gay Pinnell. *Guided Reading*. London: Heinemann, 1996.

Gambrell, Linda B., Lesley Mandel Morrow, and Michael Pressley, eds. *Best Practices in Literacy Instruction*. 3rd ed. New York: Guilford Press, 2007.

Harvey II, Carl A. "Leveling for Leverage." *Library Media Connection* January 2006: 42-43.

Jurenka, Nancy Allen. *Teaching Phonemic Awareness through Children's Literature and Experiences*. Westport, CT: Teacher Ideas Press, 2005.

Kletzien, Sharon Benge, and Mariam Dreher. *Informational Text in K-3 Classrooms*. Newark: International Reading Association, 2003.

Knowles, Elizabeth, and Martha Smith. *Boys and Literacy: Practical Strategies for Librarians, Teachers, and Parents*. Westport, CT: Libraries Unlimited, 2005.

Krashen, Stephen. *The Power of Reading*. 2nd ed. Littleton: Libraries Unlimited, 2004.

Laminack, Lester L., and Reba M. Wadsworth. *Reading Aloud Across the Curriculum*. Portsmouth, NH: Heinemann, 2006.

Lance, Keith Curry, et al. *Information Empowered: The School Librarian as an Agent of Academic Achievement in Alaska Schools*. Anchorage, AK: Alaska State Library, 1999.

Moreillon, Judi. *Collaborative Strategies for Teaching Reading Comprehension*. Chicago: American Library Association, 2007.

Pearson, P. David. "Thinking About the Reading/Writing Connection." *Voices* March/April 2002.

Pitcher, Sharon, M., and Bonnie Mackey. *Collaborating for Real Literacy: Librarian, Teacher, and Principal*. Worthington, OH: Linworth Publishing, Inc., 2004.

Preddy, Leslie B. *SSR with Intervention*. Westport, CT: Libraries Unlimited, 2007.

Report of the National Reading Panel. Washington, DC: National Institute of Child Health and Human Development, 2000.

Ross, Catherine, and Paulette M. Rothbauer. *Reading Matters*. Littleton: Libraries Unlimited, 2005.

Simpson, Carol. *Copyright for Schools: A Practical Guide*. 4th ed. Worthington, OH: Linworth Publishing, Inc., 2005.

Smith, Michael, and Jeffrey Wilhelm. *Reading Don't Fix No Chevys*. London: Heinemann, 2002.

Todd, Ross J., Carol C. Kuhlthau, and OELMA. *Student Learning through Ohio School Libraries: The Ohio Research Study*. Columbus, OH: Ohio Educational Library Media Association, 2004.

Tovani, Cris. *Do I Really Have to Teach Reading?* New York: Stenhouse Publishers, 2004.

Trelease, Jim. *The Read-Aloud Handbook: Sixth Edition*. New York: Penguin, 2006.

Walker, Christine, and Sarah Shaw. *Teaching Reading Strategies in the School Library*. Littleton: Libraries Unlimited, 2004.

Weissman, Annie. *Transforming Storytimes into Reading and Writing Lessons*. Worthington, OH: Linworth Publishing, Inc., 2001.

Wood, Julie. *Literacy Online*. Portsmouth, NH: Heinemann, 2004.

WEB RESOURCES

Information Power
   <www.ala.org/aaslTemplate.cfm?Section=informationpowerbook>
International Reading Association
   <www.reading.org>

National Council of Teachers of English
\<www.ncte.org\>
Read, Write, Think
\<http://readwritethink.org\>
Reading Rockets
\<www.readingrockets.org\>

CHAPTER 4

MATHEMATICS

SCHOOL IMPROVEMENT SNAPSHOT

Back at Parrott Elementary, Karen Knapp, library media specialist and James Matthews, 5th grade teacher, are in a planning session.

Karen: So, you are getting ready to talk about explorers and want to create a project for your students to have some real-world experiences about being explorers.

James: Right. I want to help them make connections from what explorers had to do to plan a trip to what students would have to do today to plan a trip.

Karen: Aha. So the students could actually plan their spring break vacation for their family?

James: Yes. Oh, I like that. It will help us compare their efforts for planning a trip to that of what explorers in the 18th and 19th century had to do.

Karen: You know, I think we could even expand this beyond social studies. The trip is going to cover a lot of math skills. The children are going to have to work with money and use addition and multiplication to figure out total costs, and we could even have them set it all up in a spreadsheet on the computer. One of our school improvement goals is computation – especially helping students improve their multiplication skills, so this will be a perfect way to give them practice in a real-world experience.

James: The fifth grade math standards have students mastering multiplication, too. Let's get the library media schedule out and see how much time we think we'll need to do this project.

Karen and James' conversation is a perfect example of how mathematics can be incorporated into an information literacy project.

DEFINITION

In addition to literacy, one of the other major focuses of school improvement is on mathematics. As with literacy, all students are to be proficient in this core subject. A quick scan of state standards from across the country and the National Council of Teachers of Mathematics, shows patterns in the major headings and groupings of mathematic standards. For the purposes of this book, math will be grouped into the following categories:

NUMBER SENSE

Numbers are at the heart of math. They are used in all areas of mathematical study. Number sense is a student's ability to naturally break down numbers, use numbers as referents, and solve problems using knowledge of the base-10 system and the relationship among operations.

COMPUTATION

Computation is using mathematics to solve the answer to a problem. This includes mental calculations, estimation, and paper-pencil calculations.

ALGEBRA

Algebra is the ability to understand patterns, relationships, and functions. Algebra also includes solving mathematical situations using algebraic symbols.

GEOMETRY

Geometry involves relationship of shapes. Students should be able to analyze the characteristics and properties of shapes and use that information to solve problems.

MEASUREMENT

Students should be able to measure objects using units, systems, and processes of measurement. They should also be able to use tools and formulas to determine the measurement.

DATA ANALYSIS

Students should be able to collect, analyze, and make sense of data. They should be able to display the relevant data and answer questions about it. Students should be able to predict and infer based on data.

PROBLEM SOLVING

Problem solving is the process of using a step-by-step method to solve a mathematical problem when the answer is not known in advance. There are a multitude of strategies for findings the solution to these problems.

TRIGONOMETRY OR CALCULUS

As students move to high school, they may build on the concepts listed above and then take specialized courses such as trigonometry or calculus.

None of these areas can be taught in isolation, but rather are interdependent on each other as students progress. Student understanding of the relationship among all these areas will also be important.

INSTRUCTION

The library media specialist should be keenly aware of how math is taught in the building. Some questions library media specialists might ask about teaching mathematics in their schools are:

- What does the library media specialist know about teaching mathematics?
- What does the library media specialist know about how mathematics is taught in his/her building?
- How can the library media program make an impact on mathematics instruction?

MATCH MAKER

Many of the ways the library media specialist can help with mathematics is to provide real-world data and opportunities to apply the skills being learned. When students can see how the knowledge they are gaining can be used in their daily lives, there is more meaning to the instruction. How can math help students in managing their finances or buying a car? How can math help them repair or fix something around their house? How can the data help them make a case for their point of view? Students can see the math skills with real-world application.

Data found in the library media center also may open the door for multi-subject projects. The library media specialist can be the link for bringing a math teacher, a social studies teacher, and a language arts teacher together to see how one project can include many of the standards that all three teachers need to cover.

SPECIAL INTEREST GROUPS

Collection development will be helpful when working with special education students and English language learners. Can the library media specialist find resources to help them understand the mathematical concepts? When working with mathematics teachers, can the library media specialist offer suggestions on strategies to help these students with their projects?

STRATEGIES

Based on our definitions of the areas in mathematical study, the ideas that will follow are some examples of what a library media specialist can do to teach math. It is not meant to be all-inclusive, but rather to offer some examples to get the mind started so that library media specialists can tailor these and/or create their own ideas to their specific buildings.

NUMBER SENSE

In working with numbers, one obvious and simple connection to the library media center is the Dewey Decimal System. Perhaps when students are working on decimals, the students could come to the library and help organize or shelve books that have been returned. For example, at one school there was a student who was working in the library organizing a cart of books. As he came across situations where he was unsure where the book went in the cart, together he and the library media specialist went through all the various scenarios about putting the books in order based on the numbers. It provided him a real-world application of using numbers with decimals.

Another idea is to read aloud number books and counting books to students. For example take Doreen Cronin's *Click, Clack, Splish, Splash* and read it aloud to students. Spend time talking about numbers in the book. In total, how many fish do the animals rescue? Then with older students take it up a notch. Ask some questions such as how many more fish would they rescue if they counted by 2's, 5's, or 10's?

Just as there are many alphabet books on all types of topics, students could also create their own number book based on objects in the classroom, library, school, etc. Make a display of counting books that children can check out. They will enjoy finding other stories with numbers. Encourage the students to share what they learn in the story. This will reinforce not only comprehension strategies but also mathematical concepts!

NUMBER SENSE BIBLIOGRAPHY

Clements, Andrew. *A Million Dots*. New York: Simon & Schuster Books for Young Readers, 2006.

Cronin, Doreen, and Betsy Lewin. *Click, Clack, Splish, Splash: A Counting Adventure*. New York: Atheneum Books for Young Readers, 2006.

Dehaene, Stanislas. *The Number Sense: How the Mind Creates Mathematics*. New York: Oxford University Press, 1997.

Fisher, Valorie. *How High Can a Dinosaur Count?: and Other Math Mysteries*. New York: Schwartz & Wade Books, 2006.

Franco, Betsy. *Counting Our Way to the 100th Day!: 100 poems*. New York: Margaret K. McElderry Books, 2004.

Goldstone, Bruce. *Ten Friends*. New York: Henry Holt, 2001.

Murphy, Stuart J. *100 Days of Cool*. New York: HarperCollins Publishers, 2004.

Murphy, Stuart J. *Earth Day – Hooray!* New York: HarperCollins, 2004.

Murphy, Stuart J. *Less than Zero*. New York: HarperCollins Publishers, 2003.

Murphy, Stuart J. *Missing Mittens*. New York: HarperCollins, 2001.

Nagda, Ann W., and Cindy Bickel. *Polar Bear Math: Learning about Fractions from Klondike and Snow*. New York: H. Holt and Co., 2004.

Pallotta, Jerry. *Ocean Counting: Odd Numbers*. Watertown, MA: Charlesbridge, 2005.

Pallotta, Jerry. *The Hershey's Milk Chocolate Bar Fractions Book*. New York: Scholastic, 1999.

Sayre, April P., and Jeff Sayre. *One is a Snail, Ten is a Crab: A Counting by Feet Book*. Cambridge, MA: Candlewick Press, 2003.

Scotton, Rob. *Russell the Sheep*. New York: HarperCollins, 2005.

Shahan, Sherry. *Cool Cats Counting*. Little Rock, AR: August House LittleFolk, 2005.

Tang, Greg. *Math Fables*. New York: Scholastic, 2004.

Tang, Greg. *Math-terpieces: The Art of Problem-Solving*. New York: Scholastic, 2003.

Wood, Audrey. *Ten Little Fish*. New York: Blue Sky Press, 2004.

COMPUTATION

Barb Engvall from John Campbell Elementary in Selah, Washington, has her students tally the votes for their state student choice award. She is modeling this with her kindergarten and first grade students, but her second and third graders are doing the tallying themselves. They are adding all the votes together before entering them on a spreadsheet.

Another idea is to set up a math center in the library media center. This could be an activity for students who have finished checking out books or who might visit the library media center during recess. One of the activities available could be a game with a set of dice. Students roll the dice, and they either have to add, subtract, multiply, or divide the numbers depending on what would be age-appropriate.

Use math to set up groups in the library media center. When the library media specialist wants students working in partners or small groups, give half the class the answer to a math problem and the other class the math problem. They have to match up to find their partner.

COMPUTATION BIBLIOGRAPHY

Calvert, Pam. *Multiplying Menace: The Revenge of Rumpel-stiltskin: a Math Adventure*. Watertown, MA: Charlesbridge, 2006.

Cobb, Annie. *The Long Wait*. New York: Kane Press, 2000.

Dalton, Julie. *Farmer's Market Rounding*. New York: Children's Press, 2007.

Dodds, Dayle A. *Minnie's Diner: A Multiplying Menu*. Cambridge, MA: Candlewick Press, 2004.

Fromental, Jean-Luc, and Joëlle Jolivet. *365 Penguins*. New York: Abrams Books for Young Readers, 2006.

Mills, Claudia. *7 x 9 = Trouble!* New York: Farrar Straus Giroux, 2002.

Murphy, Stuart J. *Animals on Board*. New York: HarperCollins, 1998.

Murphy, Stuart J. *Betcha!* New York: HarperCollins Publishers, 1997.

Murphy, Stuart J. *Divide and Ride*. New York: HarperCollins, 1997.

Murphy, Stuart J. *Double the Ducks*. New York: HarperCollins, 2003.

Murphy, Stuart J. *Too Many Kangaroo Things to Do!* New York: HarperCollins, 1996.

Pinczes, Elinor J. *A Remainder of One*. Boston: Houghton Mifflin, 1995.

Scott, Janine. *Take a Guess: a Look at Estimation*. Minneapolis, MN: Compass Point Books, 2003.

Stamper, Judith B. *The Bowwow Bake Sale*. New York: Grosset & Dunlap, 2002.

Stamper, Judith B., and Chris L. Demarest. *Go, Fractions!* New York: Grosset & Dunlap, 2003.

VanVoorst, Jennifer. *Can You Guess?* Mankato, MN: Yellow Umbrella Books, 2004.

Wingard-Nelson, Rebecca. *Addition Made Easy*. Berkeley Heights, NJ: Enslow Elementary, 2005.

Wingard-Nelson, Rebecca. *Subtraction Made Easy*. Berkeley Heights, NJ: Enslow Elementary, 2005.

Ziefert, Harriet. *Rabbit and Hare Divide an Apple*. New York: Viking, 1998.

Zuravicky, Orli. *Amazing Animals: Multiplying Multidigit Numbers by One Digit Numbers with Regrouping*. New York: PowerKids Press, 2004.

ALGEBRA

★ *Students could research the history of algebra and create a timeline demon-strating some of the major discoveries about algebra over the years. This project could be done at the beginning of the year to give students a preview of what they will be learning. As each skill was introduced, the class could refer back to the research about the major events in mathematics. It could also be a reflective assign-ment to do at the end of the year when students could summarize all they have learned by figuring out when mathematical strategies were discovered. The library media specialist and teacher would work together to help students find appropriate and authoritative sources for the project.*

Middle or high school students could choose one of the books by Stuart J. Murphy to read that explains a simple concept of algebra. Students would then work to create their own book to share with elementary students. It would be important that they use simple algebra so that elementary students would under-stand it, and that the story they write correctly explains the concept.

Use the library media center facility as a mathematical problem for students. One scenario could be that the library media center is moving to a new facility. They have so many books, so many audiobooks, magazines, etc. and then give them numbers of items that will fit on a shelf. Students then can determine how many shelves the new library media center might need.

ALGEBRA BIBLIOGRAPHY

Caron, Lucille, and Philip M. St. Jacques. *Pre-Algebra and Algebra*. Berkeley Heights, NJ: Enslow Publishers, 2000.

Guillen, Michael. *Five Equations that Changed the World: The Power and Poetry of Mathematics*. New York: Hyperion, 1995.

Murphy, Stuart J. *3 Little Firefighters*. New York: HarperCollins, 2003.

Murphy, Stuart J. *Dave's Down-to-Earth Rock Shop*. New York: HarperCollins, 2000.

Murphy, Stuart J. *Dinosaur Deals*. New York: HarperCollins, 2001.

Murphy, Stuart J. *A Pair of Socks*. New York: HarperCollins, 1996.

Murphy, Stuart J. *Ready, Set, Hop!* New York: HarperCollins, 1996.

Packard, Edward. *Big Numbers: And Pictures That Show Just How Big They Are*. Brookfield, CT: Millbrook Press, 2000.

Tabak, John. *Algebra: Sets, Symbols, And the Language of Thought*. New York: Facts On File, 2004.

GEOMETRY

★ *The art of creating a picture book is a talent. Many of today's great illustrators use a variety of techniques and processes to create their illustrations. Working with the art teacher and the math teacher, the library media specialist could provide examples of picture books where students could look to find basic geometric shapes, symmetry, angles, etc. Discovering what shapes and lines are the basis for the illustrations can be used to help students as they create their own illustrations.*

Use the die-cut machine and cut out several shapes. Have students go on a "hunt" throughout the library to see how may different places they could find their shape in the library media center. Or, have students get in groups and see if they can combine their shapes to make something people would recognize.

Tangrams are another great use of shapes. Have sets available for student to check out with books such as *Grandfather Tang's Story* by Ann Tompert or *Tangram Magic* by Lisa Campbell Ernst. These could also be included in a good math center in the library media center.

For older students, they might explore the world of M.C. Escher. His amazing artwork can be a catalyst for discussion on why and how tessellations work. Students could divide into two groups. One group could research Escher's life and inspirations and another group could research the history of tessellations. The two groups would then be responsible for teaching the class what they found.

GEOMETRY BIBLIOGRAPHY

Adler, David A. *Shape Up!* New York: Holiday House, 1998.
Campbell, Kathy K. *Let's Draw a Fish with Triangles*.
    New York: PowerStart Press, 2004.
Chappell, Rachel M. *Geometry at Every Turn*. Vero Beach, FL:
    Rourke Pub, 2007.
Ehlert, Lois. *Color Farm*. New York: Lippincott, 1990.
Ehlert, Lois. *Color Zoo*. New York: HarperCollins, 1989.
Leake, Diyan. *Circles*. Chicago: Raintree, 2006.
Leake, Diyan. *Triangles*. Chicago: Raintree, 2006.
Metropolitan Museum of Art. *Museum Shapes*. New York: Little, Brown,
    2005.
Murphy, Chuck. *Shapes*. New York: Little Simon, 2001.
Murphy, Stuart J. *Let's Fly a Kite*. New York: HarperCollins, 2000.
Murphy, Stuart J., and Edward Miller. *Circus Shapes*. New York:
    HarperCollins, 1998.

Neuschwander, Cindy. *Sir Cumference and the Sword in the Cone*. Watertown, MA: Charlesbridge, 2003.

Olson, Nathan. *Squares Around Town*. Mankato, MN: Capstone Press, 2007.

Olson, Nathan. *Triangles Around Town*. Mankato, MN: Capstone Press, 2007.

Pallotta, Jerry. *Twizzlers Shapes and Patterns*. New York: Scholastic, 2002.

Petelinsek, Kathleen, and E. R. Primm. *Colors and Shapes: Colores y formas*. Chanhassen, MN: Child's World, 2005.

Randolph, Joanne. *Let's Draw a Bird with Shapes*. New York: PowerStart Press, 2005.

Rau, Dana M. *A Star in My Orange: Looking for Nature's Shapes*. Brookfield, CT: Millbrook Press, 2002.

Ribke, Simone T. *The Shapes We Eat*. New York: Children's Press, 2004.

Ros, Jordina, and Pere Estadella. *Fun Crafts with Shapes*. Berkeley Heights, NJ: Enslow Elementary, 2006.

Weber, Rebecca. *Building With Shapes*. Minneapolis, MN: Compass Point Books, 2005.

Weekly Reader Early Learning Library. *I Know Shapes*. Milwaukee: Weekly Reader Early Learning Library, 2006.

Woodford, Chris. *Area*. Detroit: Blackbirch Press, 2005.

MEASUREMENT

★ *Recipes are always a popular topic with students because they connect with food. Many of today's popular chefs not only have written books for adults but also for children. Reading and cooking with recipes is a good way to teach measurement to students. Library media specialists can help students locate recipes online or in the print collection. Using the recipes, students can experiment to see what happens when ingredients are left out or when too much or too little of an ingredient is put in the mix. In elementary schools this would be the perfect opportunity to partner with the cafeteria staff. At the secondary level, it would be the perfect opportunity to collaborate with the Family and Consumer Science teacher. Recording and organizing this information could be done with spreadsheet software.*

Use the library media center as a measuring adventure. How many feet are the shelves? Inches? How many centimeters from the circulation desk to the front door? How many yards are the story steps? The library media center facility has a plethora of objects and areas that could be measured. Older students could measure them and then work to convert them to a scale for making a map.

Use measurement to give student perspective. When a class researches animals, have them create a life-size picture of the animal. Use Steve Jenkin's *Actual Size* as an introduction to that assignment. Students could then make their own version of his tale based on the measurements from their research.

MEASUREMENT BIBLIOGRAPHY

Henshaw, John M. *Does Measurement Measure Up?: How Numbers Reveal and Conceal the Truth*. Baltimore: Johns Hopkins University Press, 2006.

Lagasse, Emeril. *Emeril's There's a Chef in My Soup!: Recipes for the Kid in Everyone*. New York: HarperCollins, 2002.

Lagasse, Emeril. *Emeril's There's a Chef in My World!: Recipes that Take You Places*. New York: HarperCollins, 2006.

Leedy, Loreen. *Measuring Penny*. New York: Henry Holt, 1997.

Linde, Barbara M. *Building Washington, D.C.: Measuring the Area of Rectangular Shapes*. New York: PowerKids Press, 2004.

Loughran, Donna. *How Long Is It?* New York: Children's Press, 2004.

Murphy, Stuart J. *Polly's Pen Pal*. New York: HarperCollins, 2005.

Murphy, Stuart J. *Room for Ripley*. New York: HarperCollins, 1999.

Murphy, Stuart J. *Super Sand Castle Saturday*. New York: HarperCollins, 1999.

Patilla, Peter. *Length*. North Mankato, MN: Thameside Press, 2001.

Pistoia, Sara. *Measurement*. Chanhassen, MN: Child's World, 2007.

Reisberg, Joanne A. *Zachary Zormer Shape Transformer: A Math Adventure*. Watertown, MA: Charlesbridge, 2006.

Sargent, Brian. *How Much Does It Hold?* New York: Children's Press, 2006.

Schwartz, David M. *Millions to Measure*. New York: HarperCollins, 2003.

Sullivan, Navin. *Area, Distance, and Volume*. New York: Marshall Cavendish Benchmark, 2007.

Sullivan, Navin. *Speed*. New York: Marshall Cavendish Benchmark, 2007.

Wells, Robert E. *How Do You Know What Time It Is?* Morton Grove, IL: Albert Whitman & Company, 2002.

Woodford, Chris. *Area*. Detroit: Blackbirch Press, 2005.

Woodford, Chris. *Height*. Detroit: Blackbirch Press, 2005.

DATA ANALYSIS

★ *The library media center is a wealth of data and statistics. Mathematics teachers can collaborate with almost any other department or subject to find a relative topic that would apply across the curriculum. Students can use the resources in the library media center to collect pertinent statistics and then organize those using spreadsheets or databases. The library media specialist can provide instruction on existing online databases and help students as they organize the data they have found. All of the instructors can help with teaching students to interpret the information they have found to formulate logical conclusions, findings, or predictions.*

At some point in most social studies curriculum, students study the history of their state. For example, fourth graders study Indiana history. Students could use statistics from the state and county to find out about the area in which they live. How has the population grown or decreased in the last several years? What other statistics can they find out about their area? Weather? Census? Economy? Perhaps a field trip to the town hall or public library may be needed to get all the necessary information.

Older students might research about perspective careers and colleges. What is the most cost-effective university for their intended degree? What does the current job market look like for someone coming out of college with that degree? What scholarships are available? What are the odds that they could get one of them?

DATA ANALYSIS BIBLIOGRAPHY

Clemson, Wendy, David Clemson, and Jonathan Noble. *Using Math to Win a Grand Prix*. Milwaukee, WI: Gareth Stevens Publishing, 2005.

Clemson, Wendy. *Using Math to Conquer Extreme Sports*. Milwaukee, WI: Gareth Stevens Publishing, 2005.

Estigarribia, Diana. *Learning About the Effects of Natural Events with Graphic Organizers*. New York: PowerKids Press, 2005.

Leedy, Loreen. *The Great Graph Contest*. New York: Holiday House, 2005.

Murphy, Stuart J. *Lemonade for Sale*. New York: HarperCollins Publishers, 1998.

Murphy, Stuart J. *Probably Pistachio*. New York: HarperCollins, 2001.

Nagda, Ann W., and Cindy Bickel. *Tiger Math: Learning to Graph from a Baby Tiger*. New York: Henry Holt, 2000.

PROBLEM SOLVING

★ *If one thinks about a mathematical problem and research models, one can see that many of the same steps in solving an informational problem are repeated when solving a mathematical problem. As part of that process, gaining additional information may be needed. The library media specialist and classroom teacher can work together to design problems for the students to solve that require them not only to solve it mathematically but also require them to have to look for additional information in the library media center in order to solve the problem.*

Students are assigned the task of planning for a trip. They are given a specific destination and a finite budget. They have to research and determine how to travel, where to stay, what to eat, etc., to stay within their budget. Not only will they have to do a great deal of math but they will also have to do some research in all those areas. This project could also be tied to social studies, and students' destinations could be someplace they are studying – their state, a country, etc.

High school students could determine how much the class has to raise to put on the senior prom. Students need to research costs, locations, and determine a fee to charge attendees. In addition, other fundraisers may be needed. The seniors could prepare a plan that takes all of those factors into consideration.

PROBLEM SOLVING BIBLIOGRAPHY

Adler, David A. *You Can, Toucan, Math: Word Problem-Solving Fun.* New York: Holiday House, 2006.

Fisher, Valorie. *How High Can a Dinosaur Count?: And Other Math Mysteries.* New York: Schwartz & Wade Books, 2006.

Guillen, Michael. *Five Equations that Changed the World: The Power and Poetry of Mathematics.* New York: Hyperion, 1995.

Keenan, Sheila, and Marilyn Burns. *Lizzy's Dizzy Day.* New York: Scholastic, 2001.

Murphy, Stuart J. *The Best Vacation Ever.* New York: HarperCollins, 1997.

Packard, Edward. *Big Numbers: And Pictures That Show Just How Big They Are!* Brookfield, CT: Millbrook Press, 2000.

Sargent, Brian. *Guess the Order.* New York: Children's Press, 2006.

Sargent, Brian. *Slumber Party Problem Solving.* New York: Children's Press, 2006.

Tang, Greg. *Math for All Seasons: Mind-Stretching Math Riddles.* New York: Scholastic Press, 2002.

Tang, Greg. *Math Potatoes: Mind-Stretching Brain Food.* New York: Scholastic Press, 2005.

Tang, Greg. *Math-terpieces: The Art of Problem-Solving.* New York: Scholastic, 2003.

Wingard-Nelson, Rebecca. *Word Problems Made Easy.* Berkeley Heights, NJ: Enslow Elementary, 2005.

TRIGONOMETRY OR CALCULUS

There are many individuals who have contributed to the field of trigonometry or calculus. Students could choose one of these individuals to research and explain their contribution to the subject they are currently studying. Students would share what led to the discoveries in trigonometry or calculus.

TRIGONOMETRY OR CALCULUS BIBLIOGRAPHY

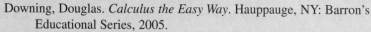

Bachman, David. *Advanced Calculus Demystified.* New York: McGraw-Hill Professional, 2007

Downing, Douglas. *Calculus the Easy Way.* Hauppauge, NY: Barron's Educational Series, 2005.

Kelley, W. Michael. *The Humongous Book of Calculus Problems.* Indianapolis: Alpha, 2007.

Miller, Bob. *Bob Miller's Precalc with Trigonometry for the Clueless.* New York: McGraw-Hill, 2005.

COLLECTION DEVELOPMENT

Perhaps one of the strongest connections the library media specialist can make with mathematics is by finding books and other materials in the library collection that can help teach the subject. Authors such as Stuart J. Murphy, Loreen Leedy, Greg Tang, and many others at the elementary level have been publishing books that cover a multitude of mathematical topics. Many of these books are great read-alouds with children and can provide an interesting way for teachers and the library media specialist to introduce mathematical concepts. Beyond books, the non-print collection can contain a multitude of manipulatives, games, and hands-on activities that can be used to reinforce mathematics. Activities such as Math Power™ games from Frog Publication <www.frog.com> allow a variety of students to play games at a station on a variety of mathematical topics.

★ On the secondary level, the collection may focus on specific mathematical topics or individuals who had an impact on the study of mathematics. A variety of reading levels will be important to help provide a balanced collection that will be useful to all students. One way to open the door to collaboration is to invite math teachers to help in selecting materials for the high school collection. These teachers will be more likely to use the resources because they had a hand in selecting it. When the materials arrive, the library media specialist can share them with the teachers and offer ideas for how they could use that resource in a collaborative project.

The Internet is also a vast resource for online practice of mathematical skills. Library media center Web sites should link to a variety of sites for students and staff to use. This can help bridge the hurdle of making connections between mathematics and the library media center.

REFLECTION

Mathematics is a major part of school improvement since it is one of the two major areas in *No Child Left Behind* (NCLB). All teachers are stressed about testing and the scores that reflect on them. A library media specialist who is well versed in the standards and the resources available, and who has a persistent personality to consistently offer ideas and suggestions for projects and units will certainly be able to open the door to collaboration with the math department. When working collaboratively, social studies, science, and English easily can find connections to one another through the library. The library media specialist can help by making those connections with mathematics, too.

PROFESSIONAL RESOURCES

Buzzeo, Toni. *Collaborating to Meet Standards K-6.* 2nd ed. Worthington, OH: Linworth Publishing, Inc., 2007.

Chambers, Donald. *Putting Research into Practice in the Elementary Grades.* Reston, VA: National Council of Teachers of Mathematics, 2002.

Laminack, Lester, and Reba M. Wadsworth. *Reading Aloud across the Curriculum.* London: Heinemann, 2006.

Lester, Frank. *Teaching Mathematics through Problem Solving.* Urbana: National Council of Teachers of English, 2003.

MacDonell, Colleen. *Project-Based Inquiry Units for Young Children.* Worthington, OH: Linworth Publishing, Inc., 2006.

Small, Marian, and Carole E. Greenes. *Navigating Through Problem Solving and Reasoning.* Reston, VA: National Council of Teachers of Mathematics, 2004.

Thiessen, Diane. *Exploring Mathematics through Literature.* Reston, VA: National Council of Teachers of Mathematics, 2004.

Zemelman, Steven, Harvey Daniels, and Arthur Hyde. *Best Practice.* London: Heinemann, 1998.

Web Resources

AAA Math
    < www.aaamath.com/>
FunBrain.com
    <www.funbrain.com>
Harcourt Multimedia Math Glossary
    <www.hbschool.com/glossary/math2/index1.html>
Illuminations
    <http://illuminations.nctm.org/>
The Math Forum @ Drexel
National Council of Teacher of Mathematics

CHAPTER 5

TECHNOLOGY INTEGRATION

SCHOOL IMPROVEMENT SNAPSHOT

Karen Knapp, library media specialist, and Susan Vincent, principal, are talking about technology integration at Parrott Elementary.

Susan: Karen, what kind of experience do we provide our students in using technology?

Karen: I think we do a reasonably good job of creating projects that give our students ample opportunities to use technology.

Susan: I thought so too, but the middle school is clamoring that they want the students to be more proficient users of technology when they enter their building. Do you have any ideas on how we can improve our technology integration?

Karen: Perhaps we need to map out what projects our students are involved in each year and then determine if there are gaps. While we perceive we are doing a good job, maybe we need to look at some data to confirm. Working with the teaching staff, we can locate areas in the curriculum where technology makes a logical fit rather than just trying to cram it in someplace.

Susan: I think that could work. I also think we need to assess what professional development we could offer teachers to help them integrate technology. We have a lot of resources here at Parrott Elementary. It is important that we use them effectively and efficiently for the benefit of our students.

Karen: Absolutely. I'll call a meeting of the Media/Technology Advisory Committee to start collecting information.

M ost library media specialists have long been on the bandwagon to help integrate technology into instruction. Since the "media" in schools often resided in the library, librarians were the ones who had to determine how it could best be used for instruction and then model that use when working with teachers and students.

Definition

As part of *No Child Left Behind* (NCLB), students are required by eighth grade to be deemed proficient technology users. NCLB does not define a proficient technology user but rather leaves that to each state to determine. Each state also determines how and in what form information will be collected regarding students as proficient technology users. Many states have either based the definition on their own standards or used the National Educational Technology Standards (NETS) created by the International Society for Technology in Education (ISTE), <http://www.iste.org/Template.cfm?Section=NETS>. The newest version of the NETS for Students Standards was released in July 2007.

Instruction

What impact do these technology standards have on instruction? What role can the library media specialist play? Many of the elements included in the definitions a state may adopt transfer to information literacy. Students will need to be able to find, evaluate, and create information. Students have access to a vast amount of digital resources to find information and technology tools to create information. Library media specialists can help provide students with guidance on how these digital resources and tools operate and help teach them to be competent users. Technology integration provides yet another opportunity for collaboration between classroom teachers and the library media specialist. Working together, they can design projects and instruction that will put students on the path to being technologically proficient.

STRATEGIES

There are a multitude of books, blogs, Web sites, etc., that can give library media specialists a more focused look at instructional strategies that will help with technology. Even more important, however, is the need for the library media specialist to model using technology when giving instruction and embed it within the lesson. Modeling will help teachers see ways they can integrate technology effectively. Library media specialists also need to be proactive in helping teachers see ways to use technology before, during, and after a project. Students can use technology to brainstorm topics and create questions using software such as Kidspiration™. They can use a wiki, a collaborative Web page designed to have multiple authors, as a way to work together on a group project. Their final product could be a multimedia slide show presentation, a digital video, or maybe a Web site linking to their wiki and asking for comments to be posted on a blog. The possibilities are endless as the Web 2.0 movement continues to provide a plethora of tools to use online with students and staff.

MANAGING SCHOOL IMPROVEMENT

Technology can help manage school improvement. One school uses an internal blog to track their school improvement plan. The blog requires a login for access. Each grade level meets in their Professional Learning Community (PLC) each week and posts to the blog for everyone to read what their grade level is doing and how it is impacting school improvement. The principal, with the assistance of the library media specialist, developed a template format for teachers to fill out and upload to the blog each week.

Not only are conversations on the blog tracking school improvement, but also the blog becomes the source where all the data is posted. It makes it a quick and easy source for staff to find when they need to access it.

Wikis also provide a collaborative environment where groups like the school improvement committee could work when writing or revising the school improvement plan. Grade levels could also organize their PLC minutes or notes on a Wiki as well. A ning is another source where collaborative communication could happen, or perhaps develop a school-wide book study where staff can share comments and ideas on the wiki, blog, or ning? As new tools are developed for Web 2.0, it is certain that library media specialists can help find ways to use them not only with students but also teachers.

ETHICS

Another major contribution that library media specialists can make is to help students and staffs become ethical users of these new tools and resources. Plagiarism and copyright violations can be a danger in some of these online environments. Library media specialists can provide instruction on effective ways to cite sources and give credit to the original author. Library media specialists can also educate about information that requires permission to be used before a student or staff member puts it on the Web.

COLLECTION DEVELOPMENT

The collection development component to technology integration requires providing the tools and resources students and teachers can use to access digital information. The library media specialist can:

- Provide pathfinders – guides to both print and non-print resources – to help guide students to online resources that will best meet their needs.
- Provide links on library media Web sites to sources of information.
- Obtain and use subscriptions to online databases students can search.
- Provide streaming video and other multimedia for students to use for information.
- Add books and periodicals to the professional collection.

There is rich content available online both free and for subscription. When working on collection development, the library media specialist will want to make sure that the library/school Web site is a portal to help students find information and use both online and print resources effectively.

REFLECTION

Technology is an ever-changing tool used in education today. Library media specialists should be at the forefront of working with teachers and students to effectively use technology. Technology is just one tool that educators have at their disposal, but as it continues to be a bigger factor in the lives of today's students, it will be more and more important for schools to utilize technology as a seamless part of instruction. As schools look for opportunities to motivate students to learn, technology will play a crucial role in making connections with students. School improvement plans and NCLB are all requiring students to use the technology tools available. Library media specialists can be key players in helping students and staff both learn and use technology effectively.

PROFESSIONAL RESOURCES

Baule, Steven. *Case Studies in Educational Technology and Library Leadership.* Worthington, OH: Linworth Publishing, Inc., 2005.

Baule, Steven. *Technology Planning for Effective Teaching and Learning.* 2nd ed. Worthington, OH: Linworth Publishing, Inc, 2001.

Bell, Ann. *Handheld Computers in Schools and Media Centers.* Worthington, OH: Linworth Publishing, Inc., 2007.

Church, Audrey. *Your Library Goes Virtual.* Worthington, OH: Linworth Publishing, Inc., 2007.

Conover, Patricia Ross. *Technology Projects for Library Media Specialists and Teachers.* Worthington, OH: Linworth Publishing, Inc., 2007.

Johnson, Doug. *Learning Right from Wrong in the Digital Age: An Ethics Guide for Parents, Teachers, Librarians, and Others Who Care about Computer-Using Young People.* Worthington, OH: Linworth Publishing, Inc., 2003.

Richardson, Will. *Blogs, Wikis, Podcasts, and Other Powerful Web Tools for Classrooms.* Thousand Oaks: Corwin Press, 2006.

Simpson, Carol. *Copyright for Schools.* 4th ed. Worthington, OH: Linworth Publishing, Inc., 2005.

Warlick, David. *Redefining Literacy for the 21st Century.* Worthington, OH: Linworth Publishing, Inc., 2004.

WEB RESOURCES

International Society for Technology Educators
    <www.iste.org>

FREE BLOG CREATION SITES:
Blogger
    <www.blogger.com/start>
Class Blogmeister
    <http://classblogmeister.com/>
    (Designed especially for educators to use with students)
Edublogs
    <http://edublogs.org>

FREE WIKI CREATION SITES:
Peanut Butter Wiki
    <http://pbwiki.com/>
Wikispaces
    <www.wikispaces.com/>

CHAPTER **6**

DATA COLLECTION

SCHOOL IMPROVEMENT SNAPSHOT

At a school improvement committee meeting at Parrott Elementary, Karen Knapp, the library media specialist and chairperson, is talking with Laura White, a special education teacher in the building.

Karen: Laura, we noticed on the third grade standardized test that some of our students are not doing an effective job on the writing prompt.

Laura: My special education students have trouble with that part of the test as well, but we tried some new strategies with them this year. The data shows that the strategies worked. The special education scores on the writing prompt went up this year.

Karen: Do you think those same type of strategies would be effective for other students in the building as well?

Laura: Sure. I will be happy to share them with the classroom teachers. But we need to continue to collect data to make sure the strategies are working.

Karen: Sounds like a great idea to me. I can set up some spreadsheets and graphs to help us organize the information. We can continue to monitor your special education students, too, and see if they continue to improve when they take the test next year.

D ata analysis is one of the buzz phrases in today's educational system. Standardized test results are driving instruction and curriculum. The ability to interpret data becomes a hot commodity in a school. Beyond that, schools are also implementing a host of other assessments in order to monitor student achievement. Library media specialists need to be a part of the group that examines the data and determines strategies for making improvement. Data interpretation provides another avenue for determining where the library media program can support increasing student achievement. Beyond studying school-wide data, library media specialists also must look at what they do in their library media programs and collect data to determine if their efforts are effective.

The benefits of collecting data include keeping library media specialists on course. The data provides a measuring device for evaluating the services provided by the library media center. Data validates what techniques and materials are effective and helps reveal where it would be advantageous to make some changes. As good as we are, we can always get better. Data helps paint a map toward improvement.

LIBRARY MEDIA SPECIALIST ROLE IN HELPING COLLECT DATA

Data analysis for school improvement can be broken down into two parts. The first part looks at individual students.

- In what areas is the student not succeeding?
- What additional support can we provide?
- What new strategies should we implement?

The second part looks more at the overall program.

- What trends can be seen in the data?
- Is there a consistent piece of instruction where student achievement is lacking?
- What types of changes in teaching and instruction need to be made in order to improve student performance?

Typically, looking at individual students is easier. If an individual student needs special help, it can be easy to look for a solution for that one student. Programmatic change based on looking at the overall program can be much harder. It is hard to separate people from the program. Administrative and teacher attitudes will be critical in how those changes are implemented. Data can eliminate the people factor by showing facts versus opinions. The conversations that can result from data analysis are important. The library media specialist must be a part of those discussions in order to be proactive in offering a library media program that is an integral part of increasing student achievement.

When results come back from state standardized tests, the library media specialist should take time to work with teachers and administrators to analyze the results. Be proactive and volunteer to help. The library media specialist has a whole-school perspective much like an administrator. This holistic view helps the library media specialist be more objective when looking at the instructional program of the school. Look for ways at all levels where the school library media program can help implement new strategies and techniques.

REPORTS

Reports and categories used in standardized test reports vary. Usually though, they will be grouped into common types or categories – often similar to the headings used in the state standards. Many states post sample test questions on the state department of education Web site. How does this knowledge help? As library media specialists are working with teachers to design instruction, those who have the ability and the knowledge of what areas need improvement can give instruction in these skills in the units, projects, and lessons they plan with teachers. For example, many standardized tests have informational text where students are required to answer questions or write a response. When working with teachers to plan research projects, mini-lessons designed to help students understand how to pull information from informational text will serve them not only for the project but also the test.

Beyond the standardized tests that are typically administrated once a year, most schools and districts are looking at more periodic assessment tools. These could be locally developed or purchased through various vendors, such as the Northwestern Evaluation Association (NWEA) or CTB/McGraw-Hill.

No matter what the library media specialist thinks about testing and assessment, it is important that he or she be aware of the data and utilizes those results to maximize opportunities for collaboration and working with students. Library media specialists can be the voice that shares how inquiry and project-based learning can be engaging and interesting to the learners, while preparing them to pass the test, as well.

COLLECTING LIBRARY MEDIA CENTER DATA

Since the 1992 Colorado Study, studies have been done in more than 17 states about the impact of school libraries on student achievement. While the methods and format of those studies have varied, the results have always been clear that libraries have a strong role to play in impacting student achievement.

FOR MORE INFORMATION ON THE VARIOUS RESEARCH STUDIES, GO TO:

Library Research Service
   <www.lrs.org/impact.php>
School Libraries Work
   <http://librarypublishing.scholastic.com/content/stores/LibraryStore/pages/images/SLW3—2008.pdf>

With the state studies and the standardized tests, why would library media specialists need or want to collect more data? Local data can be more powerful than national or state data when talking with local stakeholders. Qualitative data gives the stories, opinions, observations, and quotes that offer a real-life picture of the library media center. Quantitative data gives the number, statistics, and charts that provide a numeric representation of library media center programs. Often just telling someone about the library media program is not enough; at the same time, reciting statistics and showing charts does not tell the whole story, either. For example, telling a school board member or an administrator that you need more money for outdated books might fall on deaf ears. However, providing sample books from the collection that are outdated along with circulation statistics that prove these materials are not being used paints a more accurate picture of the true needs. Showing them the lack of resources to support certain projects and standards can also help make the case.

So, what kind of data should be collected? First are the traditional types of data that are often connected to the administrative role of the library media specialist:

- How many items have been checked out?
- What sections of the library have been used most? Least?
- How many classes/students visited the library? In what time period?
- How many in-services in which topics have been provided were held? For whom?
- What was the average per student weekly, monthly, or annual circulation?
- How many new items have been added to the collection?
- How many hits have there been on the computer catalog?
- How many hits have there been on the online databases?
- How was the library media center budget allocated?
- What was the per pupil library budget?
- How many times did co-planning with teachers occur?

- How much is the school library Web site used? By students and parents? By teachers?

A relatively new form of data collection gaining momentum is evaluation of student learning in the library media center. Although sometimes this means grading student work, it can also describe other means of assessing whether or not the instruction is working and what changes should be made to help those students who are struggling. Some assessment methods include:

- Rubrics – stating what categories will be assessed and giving descriptions at various levels
- Checklists – providing a list of everything the project should include
- Rating Scales – rating each item on a number scale
- Graphic Organizers – organizing information visually
- Observation – observing students as they work
- Conversations with students – interacting with students one-on-one, in small groups, or in large groups so they can demonstrate their knowledge or understanding

A third type is the data collected on library media specialist instruction and collaboration. According to the 2000 Colorado Study by Dr. Keith Curry Lance, Maria J. Rodney, and Christine Hamilton-Pennell, elementary school students with the most collaborative library media specialists scored 21 percent higher on the state assessment. Lesson plans and collaboration logs provide documentation of the subject areas and resources used to impact student learning. These statistics can guide collection development, future lesson planning, and improved co-planning. They can also tell the story of how the library media program is working to improve student achievement.

A busy library media specialist needs a plan for identifying what data and in what quantity to collect. The plan will probably be different for each and every library media program, since there are many factors that determine what data to collect: school improvement goals, library media program goals, and individual preferences of the school's current administrator. To determine what to collect, ask the following questions:

- What are the school improvement goals?
- What is the library media specialist doing in the library media center to help meet the goals?
- What evidence can the library media specialist provide to show the program is helping with those goals?
- What are the goals of the library media program?

- What evidence can the library media specialist provide to show progress towards those goals?
- How do those goals impact the overall school improvement plan?
- What are the areas of interest for the building administrator?
- What information and in what format does the building administrator prefer data?

Remember that building administrators have a major impact on the library media center program. Wise school library media specialists understand the issues and topics that are the focus of the administrator. Library media specialists keep that in mind when creating reports and collecting data.

REFLECTION

Data drives decisions. Data can keep a library media program on a flexible schedule as opposed to a fixed schedule. Data can determine the need for an increase in spending on library materials. Data can determine staffing needs. As library media programs are planned and courses are charted, school library media specialists have to determine the kinds of data to collect and how to collect them. Having a plan in place will make it easier to collect, maintain, and analyze data in order to make positive changes. Having data that demonstrates how the library media program impacts school improvement plans can have a positive effect on how the library media program is viewed in the school.

PROFESSIONAL RESOURCES

Adcock, Donald, ed. *A Planning Guide for Information Power.* Chicago: American Library Association, 1999.

Bernhardt, Victoria L. *Data Analysis.* Larchmont, NY: Eye on Education, 1998.

Church, Audrey P. *Leverage Your Library Program to Raise Test Scores.* Worthington, OH: Linworth Publishing, Inc., 2003.

Everhart, Nancy. *Evaluating the School Library Media Center: Analysis Techniques and Research Practices.* Englewood, CO: Libraries Unlimited, 1998.

Harada, Violet, and Joan Yoshina. *Assessing Learning: Librarians and Teachers as Partners.* Westport, CT: Libraries Unlimited, 2005.

Hartzell, Gary. *Building Influence for the School Librarian: Tenets, Targets, and Tactics.* Worthington, OH: Linworth Publishing, Inc., 2003.

Johnson, Doug. "A Data Mining Primer and Implications for School Library Media Specialists." *Knowledge Quest* May/June 2004.

Lance, Keith Curry, Marcia J. Rodney, and Christine Hamilton-Pennell. *How School Librarians Help Kids Achieve Standards: The Second Colorado Study.* Spring, TX: Hi Willow Research and Publishing, 2000.

DATA COLLECTION

WHO, WHAT, WHEN, WHY AND HOW DO WE COLLECT DATA FOR THE LIBRARY MEDIA PROGRAM

Data collection can be overwhelming. It is important to focus data collection to be purposeful and relevant to tell how the library media program is an indispensable part of the school. Use this chart to track your data. The WHY is the most critical question! If there is nothing of value from the data, then it may be time to stop collecting the information.

Who is collecting the data and who is the data about? (Grade Level? Subject Areas?)	What kind of data is being collected?	When is the data being collected?	Why is the data being collected? Are there connections to school improvement goals?	How is the data collected, organized, and shared?

Loertscher, David V., and Ross Todd. *We Boost Achievement!* Salt Lake City, UT: Hi Willow Research and Publishing, 2003.

McGhee, Marla W., and Barbara A. Jansen. *The Principal's Guide to a Powerful Library Media Program.* Worthington, OH: Linworth Publishing, Inc., 2005.

McGriff, Nancy, Carl A. Harvey II, and Leslie B. Preddy. "Collecting the Data." *School Library Media Activities Monthly* Feb.-June 2004.

Stripling, Barbara K., and Sandra Hughes-Hassell, eds. *Curriculum Connections Through the Library.* Westport, CT: Libraries Unlimited, 2003.

Sykes, Judith. *Action Research.* Greenwood Village, CO: Libraries Unlimited, 2002.

Young, Jr., Terrence E. "Better Data . . . Better Decisions." *Library Media Connection* January 2005.

Zmuda, Allison, Robert Kuklis, and Everett Kline. *Transforming Schools: Creating a Culture of Continuous Improvement.* Alexandria, VA: Association for Supervision and Curriculum Development, 2004.

Zmuda, Allison. "Where Does Your Authority Come From?: Empowering the Library Media Specialist as a True Partner in Student Achievement." *School Library Media Activities Monthly* Sept. 2006.

WEB RESOURCES

"Indiana Learns." Indiana Department of Education, Office of Learning Resources. **<www.indianalearns.org/>.**

Lamb, Annette, and Larry Johnson. "The School Library Media Specialist." *Eduscapes.* **<www.eduscapes.com/sms/index.html>.**

Library Research Service **<www.lrs.org/impact.php>**

McGriff, Nancy, Carl A. Harvey II, and Leslie B. Preddy. "Collecting the Data: Templates and Resources for the School Library Media Specialist." June 2002. **<www.nobl.k12.in.us/media/NorthMedia/lms/data/index.htm>**

School Libraries Work **<www.scholastic.com/librarians/printables/downloads/slw_2006.pdf>**

CHAPTER 7

PROFESSIONAL DEVELOPMENT

SCHOOL IMPROVEMENT SNAPSHOT

Grace Williams, kindergarten teacher; Margie Preston, first grade teacher; and Karen Knapp, library media specialist, are all talking about developing a plan for professional development for the next school year.

Grace: I think we should start out by listing areas that we need to have more information or knowledge about. Then, we can determine which of those will help us most towards our school improvement goals. Finally, we can then determine presenters who could share with us that information.

Margie: I think that sounds like a good idea. When I was talking with other teachers this week, we all thought we could use more training with using technology in instruction.

Grace: I agree. I also wish I had some new strategies for reading aloud with my kids. I also sometimes feel as if I am always reading the same books and wish there were a way to learn about new titles. I know others in the building feel the same way.

Margie: Exactly. Now if we look at our school improvement plan, we know a major strategy we wanted to include was using technology to reach our goals. Perhaps we can focus on using technology to teach writing since that is our major focus next year. We hope to help our kids organize their ideas for writing better. Programs like Inspiration™ or Kidspiration™ will work well to connect technology to writing. The literacy goal also talks about strategies to use when modeling reading with our students, so that should fit in well in our professional development plan.

Karen: Ladies, I think these are all great ideas. I know I can help provide some of that staff development. I have been looking at all the new titles as they have come into our library media center this year and noted ones that would be good read-alouds or focus on a specific reading skill. I also can call our technology integration specialist at the district level and work with her to design a presentation on using the technology in our building when teaching writing. She and I can work together and maybe divide the staff into smaller groups to give more one-on-one attention.

Margie: Karen that would be perfect. I knew we had come to the right place to have this discussion. Thanks for offering to help. Grace and I will get with Mrs. Vincent to schedule the trainings.

I t would be impossible for library media specialists to know everything about every topic, but Grace and Margie found out that even if Karen did not know enough to present on the topic, she could help them find just the right presenter.

DEFINITION

Professional development is a major area where the library media specialist can have an impact. Teachers' needs, levels, and backgrounds can vary greatly. Shrinking budgets have sometimes made it difficult to send people out to conferences, so many schools work to bring people into the district to provide training. They also look at the expertise already in their district to help provide staff development.

One of the first places that districts should look at when scouting out the expertise is their library media specialist. Library media specialists can share ideas, strategies, and resources as a presenter. They can help locate, arrange, and set up for presenters from other districts or groups. Just as library media specialists work to help students become better learners, they can also help teachers become better educators.

INSTRUCTION

Professional development for adults is different from teaching students. Many presenters observe that teaching teachers requires skillful and varied techniques. Adults often have side conversations, can take overly long breaks, and sometimes arrive late for in-services. Library media specialists who lead professional development opportunities need to offer interesting and provocative beginnings and must stay focused on the topic and content. Concentrate energy on those that are there to learn, and the others will come around eventually. Hands-on practice and group problem solving exercises help keep teachers engaged in learning. If designed well, adult audiences will be enthusiastic about the workshop.

When designing professional development, here are some potential questions library media specialists might ask themselves:

- Who is the audience? A specific grade level? Team? Department? Whole school?

- What is it I want the group to learn?

- Why should the group want to learn this?

- What is the format of the workshop?

- Do I need handouts?

- How long will the workshop take?

- What can we do to make it fun? Food? Theme? Music?

- What is the evaluation of the workshop?

- What kind of follow-up will we provide?

It is important that professional development is designed for the audience. How can the session be specifically tailored to the audience's needs? The more connections that can be made from what is being taught to how it applies to what the teacher does in the classroom, the more likely teachers are to take it back and implement it.

Narrowing the focus of the workshop is important. For example with technology, focusing on one piece of equipment or software and providing time to practice and use it will be more effective than spending a little bit of time on a lot of pieces of equipment. Also, making connections between the technology being learned and school improvement goals will increase interest. For example instead of "How to use the Digital Camera," the workshop might be called "Using the Digital Camera to Connect Visuals with Text." The workshop might focus on using the digital camera to take a picture of an object with the word written on a sentence strip in front of it. Then, the picture is imported into Microsoft Word™ and students have to use that word in a sentence they write.

The same types of processes and steps would be covered in each workshop with adjustments made for each grade level. Each workshop makes a direct connection to how teachers might use the technology with students.

Format of professional development is important. The same strategies library media specialists use with students are helpful in teaching adults. Opportunities to get up and move around, hands-on use of the equipment during the workshop, and time to explore and investigate are all good strategies. Just as with students, adult instruction should not be a total lecture environment.

Designing handouts will be up to the presenter as well. Handouts typically should be useful for the participant to fall back on after the workshop for help and guidance, but at the same time does not need to have everything the presenter says word for word. Reading PowerPoint slides to an audience can be pretty boring for everyone involved. Plan accordingly for time. Workshops should have enough time to cover the material, but at the same time do not fill the workshop with fluff. Get in and get out. People value their time, so make sure to advertise an end time for the workshop as well as a beginning. Start and end on time. Follow up and provide additional help for those who need it.

Have fun with workshops. If one can connect them to a theme, go for it. For example, there were four elements that needed to be covered in a half-day workshop. The elements were divided up into stations, and the staff rotated from station to station all afternoon. The principal had been using trains as a theme all year long, so the library media specialist used that theme, too. A train whistle was blown to signal time to move to the next station, and the handouts were the participants "luggage." The ticket told them which station to start at and what station to go to next. The snacks were even train cookies provided on the "dining car" – an old A/V cart. It made for a fun afternoon, and everyone enjoyed the workshop as well as learned new things at the same time. While some might find the theme a bit much, others found the theme took some of the stress and pressure away. It made them more relaxed and the training was more fun.

Evaluation is important. Get feedback to know what went well and what did not work. A short survey completed at the end of the workshop usually works best. It is also important to provide follow-up. Offer practice sessions or offer to help teachers when they are using the new strategy in their classroom for the first time. Encourage them to use these new tools during planning sessions. Library media specialists should model using new strategies in the library media center so they can see how teachers can implement them.

Strategies

⭐ *The most important thing when planning staff development is for library media specialists to demonstrate that they value people's time. Starting on time and ending on time is essential. No matter when something is offered, someone will have a conflict or others will just choose not to attend. Everyone has busy lives and schedules, so before and after-school in-services can sometimes offer challenges. Still, before or after school may be the only opportunity. Attendance may vary, but if the workshop is well planned, focused, and fun, it may compel people to attend. Successful workshops can sell themselves by word of mouth. People will not want to miss worthwhile learning opportunities in a comfortable setting.*

Another avenue is to use staff meetings. Likely these are all scheduled at the beginning of the year. Many administrators are taking staff meetings and turning them into professional development opportunities rather than times to share announcements. Library media specialists can volunteer to present during one of the meetings. The audience will already be there because they had it on their calendar, and it is a good opportunity to share something with the entire staff. Administrators are also usually happy this is one less meeting they have to plan.

Professional Development Days can also be a good opportunity to provide professional growth opportunities to staff. Library media specialists can volunteer to help plan those days and, in turn, volunteer to be a presenter. It is important, too, that when professional development is scheduled in the school that the library media specialist be a participant, too. Make sure to be vocal that the library media specialist should be included when outside presenters are brought into the building. If library media specialists are going to be able to support what teachers are doing and learning, they need to be in on the training.

Sometimes planning or prep time can be a good time for training. Because that is limited to a short amount of time, the topic has to be focused. Professional Learning Communities are another good opportunity to train teachers at a grade level because they are already meeting together anyway. The library media specialist should look for those moments where he or she can share an idea or tech tip.

COLLECTION DEVELOPMENT

In order to help foster an environment of professional development and growth, make sure the library media center's collection contains materials that will support professional development. The professional collection should be up-to-date and contain materials that support district initiatives and philosophies and help new and veteran teachers a like. This collection should be a place that teachers who are working on advanced degrees can find materials to use with their classes and for all teachers to find examples of best practices.

School improvement as a topic has a wide range of materials published from DuFour, DuFour, and Eaker's books on Professional Learning Communities to Marzano's What Works series. Many are published by the Association for Supervision and Curriculum Development. Professional journals such as *Education Leadership* and *Principal Magazine* should be available for administration and staff. It is also important to have publications from the National Council of Teachers of English and the National Council of Teachers of Math available as they connect with school improvement goals and share the latest research. The International Reading Association also publishes numerous magazines and books. Setting up this professional library could be a wonderful opportunity to partner with a building administrator or the director of curriculum. Invite them to the library media center to help weed the professional collection. At the same time, ask them for recommendations for titles that should be included in the collection. They may be able to find some funding to help support the professional collection. Grant funds, too, are a good way to add titles and resources to the professional collection. Consider writing a grant for a professional development collection.

The professional collection is not only for teachers but also library media specialists. It is important that library media specialists are reading the journals and books that administrators and teachers are reading. A library media specialist who is aware will be able to offer connections for how the library media center can fit in to the programs and ideas those magazines and books are suggesting. They can refer to the research and information available during school improvement committee meetings.

Make sure that the professional collection also contains books that support the library media specialist. Libraries Unlimited, Linworth Publishing, Inc., and others publish quality materials that will help the library media specialist grow professionally. Teachers also need to see these resources as part of the collection as it demonstrates the importance of the library media program.

Beyond print, there are many organizations that have online Web sites. Association for Supervision and Curriculum Development and others will send out weekly blasts of hot topics or headlines. Subscribe to these and pass along the information to those who will find it relevant. It is another example of a service the library media specialist can provide.

Blogs, Wikis, nings, Second Life, etc., are all online environments where educational discussions are happening. Set up an account in Google Reader or Bloglines to manage all the RSS feeds. There are many that will be useful to library media specialists and educators alike (See Figure 7.1).

LIBRARY BLOGS AND WIKIS

2¢ Worth
    <davidwarlick.com/2cents>
A Year of Reading
    <readingyear.blogspot.com/
AASL Weblog
    <www.aasl.ala.org/aaslblog>
Alan November Weblog
    <www.novemberlearning.com/blogs/alannovember/>
Alice in InfoLand
    <www.aliceinfo.org/blog/>
ASCD Blog
    <ascd.typepad.com/blog/>
Blue Skunk Blog
    <doug-johnson.squarespace.com/blue-skunk-blog/>
Deep Thinking
    <deepthinking.blogsome.com>
Digital Reshift
    <www.schoollibraryjournal.com/blog/840000284.html?nid=3367>
TeacherLibrarian Ning
From the Inside Out
    <fromtheinsideout.squarespace.com/blog/>
Gargoyles loose in the library
    <www.uni.uiuc.edu/library/blog/>
HeyJude
    <heyjude.wordpress.com>
Library Ties
    <www.carl-harvey.com/libraryties/>
ISTE's Wikispace : sigms : home

Figure 3.2

Figure 3.2 continued

Kathy Schrock's Kaffeeklatsch
    <kathyschrock.net/blog/index.htm>
Never Ending Search
    <www.schoollibraryjournal.com/blog/1340000334.html?nid=3714>
The PlanetEsme Plan: The Best New Children's Books
    <planetesme.blogspot.com/>
Practically Paradise – Diane Chen's SLJ Blog
    <www.schoollibraryjournal.com/blog/830000283.html?nid=3368>
Wanderings...
    <nlcommunities.com/communities/wanderings/default.aspx>
Weblogg-ed
    <weblogg-ed.com>

Reflction

Being active in professional development helps library media specialists be leaders in their buildings. While they may not always be the presenter, they can be connected in helping find presenters for their staff. They can also be a link to know what type of professional development is needed in their building because they work with everyone in the school. Professional development becomes another area where the library media specialist can be an active participant.

Professional Resources

Eaker, Robert, Richard DuFour, and Rebecca DuFour. *Getting Started: Reculturing Schools to Become Professional Learning Communities.* Bloomington, IN: National Educational Service, 2002.

Evans, Robert. *The Human Side of Change.* San Francisco: Jossey-Bass, 1996.

Laughlin, Sara, Denise Sisco Shockley, and Ray Wilson. *The Library's Continuous Improvement Fieldbook: 29 Ready-To-Use Tools.* Chicago: American Library Association, 2003.

Marzano, Robert J. *What Works in Schools: Translating Research into Action.* Alexandria, VA: Association for Supervision and Curriculum Development, 2003.

Wolfe, Patricia. *Brain Research: Translating Research Into Practice.* Alexandria, VA: Association for Supervision and Curriculum Development, 2001.

Zmuda, Allison, Robert Kuklis, and Everett Kline. *Transforming Schools: Creating a Culture of Continuous Improvement.* Alexandria, VA: Association for Supervision and Curriculum Development, 2004.

Web Resources

Doug Reeve's Leadership and Learning Center
    <www.makingstandardswork.com/>

CHAPTER 8

BEYOND THE SCHOOL

Walter Samuels, parent and community member, is talking with Susan Vincent, principal, and Karen Knapp, library media specialist.

Susan: Mr. Samuels, we want to review what items we use in our school to inform parents about what is happening with school improvement. We would like for you to tell us if we are on track.

Walter: Sure, I would be happy to do that.

Karen: First, we do our weekly newsletter, highlighting data from time to time, sharing successes, and asking for parents to help their children at home.

Susan: Then, we have our Web site where Karen has set up sites for both of our school goals to inform parents, give them resources to explain the goals, and provide online tools and activities they can do at home with their children.

Karen: We also had two family nights – one on math and one on literacy – where all the games and resources were focused on the two goals. All the activities were things parents could easily do at home with their children.

Walter: Yes, I have seen all of these things. I appreciate all the ways the school has to make parents a part of their school improvement efforts. Are there any other resources in the school parents can access?

Karen: Yes, we have a parent collection in the library media center that has books, videos, games, activities, etc., that parents can check out to use at home.

Walter: That is a great resource. Can we make sure to highlight that at the next PTO meeting?

K aren has done an excellent job of positioning the library media center as an important part of communicating school improvement to the parents. The Web site, parent collection, and family literacy and family math night all show the parents the active role the library media program plays in the school.

PARENT INVOLVEMENT

FAMILY NIGHT

Bringing families into the school is an important opportunity to connect school to home. Family literacy and family math nights provide a fun way for students, parents, and teachers to connect. The library media specialist can be a perfect fit for organizing such an event. Gather a group of volunteers from the staff and PTO to help put the evening together. Take volunteers from the faculty, Title I staff, district staff, etc., and ask them to work in pairs to create one simple activity. Perhaps even partner with a local university professor who could make it a class assignment to create the activities. It should be something parents could easily replicate and something that could be done in 15 minutes. The night starts with a pizza supper in the gym sponsored by the PTO or PTA. Following that, parents and students are given a list of activities happening in the building and can choose sessions to attend. By the end of the night, they should have attended three different sessions of their choice. The library media specialist could also offer sessions during that time such as recommended books, read-aloud techniques, resources in the parent collection, Web sites and online activities, etc. This is just one possibility. At the secondary level, parent night may occur without the students there and the topics might focus on homework tips, study habits, preparing for college, etc. However events like this happen in the school, the library media specialist will want to be a part of them.

LIBRARY MEDIA CENTER WEB PAGE

The library's presence on the Web should go beyond the resources collected for students and staff. Provide a direct link just for parents. Connect the links in this section to the school improvement plan. The library's computer catalog could also be linked to encourage parents to search for resources in the parent library. One component of most school improvement plans is to continue to make a connection between school and home. The library media center Web site can be one of those connections.

PARENT COLLECTION

The parent collection is another tool to bring parents into the library. Some of the things one might find in a parent library are parenting books and videos, activities, and games parents and children could do at home, and other items that would support a home-to-school connection. The parent collection at one elementary school has walkmans that students and parents can borrow to read books on tape, LeapFrog Learning Centers™ and other board games, sight-word flashcards, as well as parenting books and videos. It is funded as a joint project between the library media center and the Title I department. Grant funds are also a perfect avenue for funding such a collection. The guidance counselor and special education teachers are very good about pointing out this resource to parents during conferences and even bringing parents down to the library to point out specific resources or activities that would be helpful for their students.

FUNDING

Other outside factors to the school improvement process include sources of funding. Some may come directly through the school district while others may be outside grants. *No Child Left Behind* (NCLB) legislation comes with some funding from the federal government, but it does not fully fund all the mandates in the legislation. School districts look carefully at dollars to make sure they get the maximum use of those funds. The many studies on the impact of school libraries on student achievement show that funding of school libraries is an important part of the process. Several special programs in the U.S. Department of Education and other agencies are potential funding sources for school libraries.

READING FIRST

Reading First funding was a major source of funds in the NCLB language. Funds are distributed from the federal government to each state department of education who issues the grants based on a competitive application. The funds were to be used to improve reading instruction using research based techniques. Many school libraries have benefited from these funds while others did not. A key factor is how the grant is written, so it is important for the library media specialist to be a part of the grant writing process. Many of the grants have purchased classroom collections or leveled libraries of texts. Library media specialists can work with reading specialists and classroom teachers to share their expertise in helping with these purchases. While being seen as working on the team may not garner funds for the library, it could open the door to collaboration and perhaps further opportunities down the road.

IMPROVING LITERACY THROUGH SCHOOL LIBRARIES

Improving Literacy through School Libraries funds are distributed based on percentage of students below the poverty line. The current benchmark is 20 percent or higher. The dollars can be used for print materials to update the collection, professional development for the library media specialist, improving technology resources available in the library media center, and providing service for students beyond the school day. Advocacy efforts continue to work for increasing the funding for the grant.

OTHER GRANTS

Library media specialists should constantly be aware of grants that are available. Working with administrators and teachers to write grants to support school improvement goals is also an excellent way to increase funding for the library media center. Funding sources want to make sure their money will go to good use. They want to make sure they will make an impact on students. Helping a school reach their school improvement goals is making an impact. So writing in the grant the connections to the school improvement plan can be helpful.

REFLECTION

The community and funding go hand-in-hand. Educating the community about what the library media program does to impact instruction and, at the same time, make connections to the school improvement plan help demonstrate the library is an indispensable component to the school's success.

PROFESSIONAL RESOURCES

Anderson, Cynthia. *Write Grants, Get Money*. Worthington, OH: Linworth
Publishing, Inc., 2002.

Church, Audrey. *Your Library Goes Virtual*. Worthington, OH: Linworth Publishing,
Inc., 2007.

Hall-Ellis, Sylvia D., and Ann Jerabek. *Grants for School Libraries*. Englewood,
CO: Libraries Unlimited, 2003.

Loertscher, David V. *State Power Series: A Parent's Guide to School Libraries*.
Spring, TX: LMC Source.

WEB RESOURCES

Improving Literacy through School Libraries
   <www.ed.gov/programs/lsl/index.html>
Laura Bush Foundation
   <www.laurabushfoundation.org/>
Reading First
   <www.ed.gov/nclb/methods/reading/readingfirst.html>
Toolkit for Promoting INFOhio Resources to Parents
   <www.infohio.org/Parent/Toolkit.html>

APPENDIX A: LIBRARY MEDIA PROGRAM EVALUATION

_____ Teacher   _____ Support Staff   _____ Other

Scale: 1-4 with 1 being the lowest and 4 being the highest. If the question does not apply to your role in the building, just leave it blank.

INSTRUCTION

	1	2	3	4
1. The LMS is easily available for co-planning, co-teaching, and co-assessment.				
2. I have co-planned with the LMS this year.				
3. The LMS is proactive to suggest ideas for activities or lessons.				
4. I am comfortable going and asking the LMS for help.				
5. Students are free to come and use the LMC at anytime.				
6. The LMS regularly communicates with the staff about programming and resources using a variety of methods.				
7. The LMS provides help to me on an individual basis.				
8. The LMS provides staff development opportunities.				
9. The LMS is an integral part of the curriculum instruction at our school.				
10. The library media center provides support for reading motivation.				
11. The annual author visit is a good use of time and resources.				
12. The LMS supports my work in meeting school improvement goals.				
13. The LMS provides instruction that support school improvement goals				

14. What are (if any) stumbling blocks to using the library media specialist more to help with instruction of your students?

15. How could the LMS more effectively help you with instruction?

16. How could the library media program support the school improvement goals?

Facilities and Resources

	1	2	3	4
17. The library media center facility is welcoming and inviting.				
18. The library media center is always available when I need it.				
19. My students come at least once a week to check out new materials.				
20. I use the library media center catalog in my classroom.				
21. I use the LMC catalog with state standards search.				
22. I use video streaming resources				
23. I use electronic databases available from the LMC.				
24. The library media center has sufficient resources to meet the curriculum.				
25. The resources that are available meet my curriculum and academic standards. They are current and up-to-date.				
26. I recommended resources in our parent library to parents.				
27. I use the Leveled Library resources.				

28. In what areas (if any) do you wish the library media center could provide more resources?

29. What are stumbling blocks to accessing the available online tools?

30. What additional resources do you need to meet school improvement goals?

General Information

	1	2	3	4
31. The library facility is available for my use when needed.				
32. The library support staff is efficient in responding to your needs.				
33. The library check out/in procedures are efficient and effective.				

34. What is the most useful part of the library media program?

35. What services do you wish the library media program offered that aren't currently available?

36. List the way(s) you think the library media program could be improved to better serve students and staff.

37. What areas would you like more staff development on in the areas of media/technology?

38. Other comments/concerns/or thoughts?

Appendix B: Student Surveys

Elementary Student Survey

	YES	Not Sure	NO
1. Do you like coming to the library media center?			
2. When you come to the library media center, do you learn new things?			
3. When you come to the library media center can you get answers to your questions?			
4. When you come to the library media center, do you learn how to find information?			
5. Can you find books you want to read in our library media center?			
6. Can you find books to answer your questions in our library media center?			
7. Do you use the library media center webpage?			

8. What do you like best about the library media center?

9. If you could change one thing about our library media center, what would it be?

Secondary Study Survey – Answer the questions below. Please give examples to prove your answer.

1. What are the things in our library media center that make you want to come here to study, learn, read, use technology, and socialize?

2. When you come to the library media center who or what helps you most as you search for answers to your questions?

3. When you come to the library media center, which types of technology and software are most helpful as you try to find information?

4. What types and subjects of books would you like to find more of in our library media center?

5. What other technologies would you find helpful as you seek answers to your questions in our library media center?

6. What are the most helpful features of the library media center webpage? Which do you use most?

7. What do you like best about the library media center?

8. If you could change one thing about our library media center, what would it be?

Appendix C: Library Media Center Collaboration Planning & Teaching Log

Teacher(s): _____

Grade Level: _____ Planning Date: _____ Project Date: _____

Standards for 21st Century Learner	Project Description
1. Inquire, think critically, and gain knowledge. a. Skills: _____ b. Dispositions: _____ c. Responsibilities: _____ d. Self-Assessment: _____ **2. Draw conclusions, make informed decisions, apply knowledge to new situations, and create new knowledge.** a. Skills: _____ b. Dispositions: _____ c. Responsibilities: _____ d. Self-Assessment: _____ **3. Share knowledge and participate ethically and productively as members of our democratic society.** a. Skills: _____ b. Dispositions: _____ c. Responsibilities: _____ d. Self-Assessment: _____ **4. Pursue personal and aesthetic growth.** a. Skills: _____ b. Dispositions: _____ c. Responsibilities: _____ d. Self-Assessment: _____	
Academic Standards	**Teacher will:**
School Improvement Goals Supported / Strategies Implemented	
Resources Online Resources · Video Production · Streaming Video Power Point · Multimedia Software · Scanner Word · Inspiration/Kidspiration · Other: Excel · Digital Cameras · Other: Blog/Wiki · Digital Video Cameras · Other:	**Library Media Specialist will:**
Evaluation	

Attach any other handouts, notes, or materials created for the project.

Collaboration Log © 2008, Carl A. Harvey II - http://www.carl-harvey.com
Standards above are excerpted from Standards for the 21st-Century Learner by the American Association of School Librarians, a division of the American Library Association, copyright © 2007 American Library Association. Reprinted with permission.

Index

A

Accreditation 8
Adolescent Reading 44
Algebra 58, 63
Alphabetics 27, 36
Assessment 7, 19, 29, 51, 81, 83

B

Bernhardt, Victoria 5
Brown, Benita 43

C

Collection Development 48, 69, 76, 92
Comprehension 28, 40, 42
Computation 58, 61, 62
Curriculum 16

D

Data Analysis 21, 71, 79, 80
Data Collection 21, 79-86
Draper, GeorgeAnne 40
DuFour, Rebecca 5, 92
DuFour, Richard 1, 5, 92

E

Eaker, Robert 5
Engvall, Barb 61

F

Family Night 96
Fluency 27, 37-39
Free Voluntary Reading 28, 43
Funding 97

G

Geometry 58, 64

H

High School Math Courses 59, 69
Hunt, Lisa 36

I

Improving Literacy through School
    Libraries 98-99

K

Krashen, Stephen 28-29, 43, 48

L

Library Media Center Web page 43, 45, 97
Literacy 24-55

M

Mathematics 57-71
Moore, Alda 36, 44

N

No Child Left Behind 2, 19, 70, 74, 97
Number Sense 58, 60-61

P

Parent Collection 97
Parent Involvement 96
Patchett, Sondra 48
Problem Solving 20, 59, 68
Professional Development 15, 19, 22, 87-94

R

Readers Theatre 38
Reading First 97, 99

S

School Improvement Committee 21
School Improvement Plan 19
Standards 9, 16, 33, 47, 74
State Department of Education Web sites 4

T

Technology Integration 19, 22, 73-77
Tetrick, Gwen 45

W

Writing 20, 29, 31, 35, 45-46